ArtScroll Series®

Rabbi Nosson Scherman / Rabbi Meir Zlotowitz

General Editors

*Ideas and stories
to keep you going
when you're happy
and pick you up
when you're down*

Over 100 teenage girls
share their stories

Published by
Mesorah Publications, ltd

A GIFT -for- TEENS

Roiza D. Weinreich

FIRST EDITION
First Impression ... September 2000

Published and Distributed by
MESORAH PUBLICATIONS, LTD.
4401 Second Avenue / Brooklyn, N.Y 11232

Distributed in Europe by
LEHMANNS
Unit E, Viking Industrial Park
Rolling Mill Road
Jarrow, Tyne & Wear, NE32 3DP
England

Distributed in Israel by
SIFRIATI / A. GITLER
10 Hashomer Street
Bnei Brak 51361

Distributed in Australia and New Zealand by
GOLDS WORLD OF JUDAICA
3-13 William Street
Balaclava, Melbourne 3183
Victoria Australia

Distributed in South Africa by
KOLLEL BOOKSHOP
Shop 8A Norwood Hypermarket
Norwood 2196, Johannesburg, South Africa

ARTSCROLL SERIES®
A GIFT FOR TEENS
© Copyright 2000, by MESORAH PUBLICATIONS, Ltd. and Mrs. Roiza D. Weinreich
4401 Second Avenue / Brooklyn, N.Y. 11232 / (718) 921-9000 / www.artscroll.com

---

ALL RIGHTS RESERVED
The text, prefatory and associated textual contents and introductions
— including the typographic layout, cover artwork and ornamental graphics —
have been designed, edited and revised as to content, form and style.

No part of this book may be reproduced
IN ANY FORM, PHOTOCOPYING, OR COMPUTER RETRIEVAL SYSTEMS
— even for personal use without written permission from
the copyright holder, Mesorah Publications Ltd.
except by a reviewer who wishes to quote brief passages
in connection with a review written for inclusion in magazines or newspapers.

THE RIGHTS OF THE COPYRIGHT HOLDER WILL BE STRICTLY ENFORCED.

ISBN:
1-57819-573-X (hard cover)
1-57819-574-8 (paperback)

Typography by CompuScribe at ArtScroll Studios, Ltd.
Printed in the United States of America by Noble Book Press Corp.
Bound by Sefercraft, Quality Bookbinders, Ltd., Brooklyn N.Y. 11232

מאטיל בת ר׳ משה הלוי
נר אלקים נשמת אדם

Babunya's inextinguishable *bitachon* was symbolized by the *neiros* she lit every Friday night in the concentration camp.

Her inner strength in the most trying of times was coupled with a determination never to give up.

I remember her summer visits. Whenever she had a spare moment there was an open *Tehillim* in front of her.

Her shining example kindled and ignited the spark of Yiddishkeit in those around her.

Table of Contents

Dear Friend	9

Gratitude

Gratitude	13
A Gratitude Journal	14
Enjoy This Moment	20
The Gratitude State	21
Hashem Will Take Care Of You!	24
Wake Up And See	26
Mother	28
Food Is A Delight	30
Bread	35
Honoring Hashem	38
A Bottle Of Wine	39
Beyond Marble Cake	40
The Secret Ingredient	42
Thorns Have Roses!	44
What Do You Do When Things Go Wrong?	47
Coping During a Crisis	51
Harmony	52
Sharing the Pain	54
Attitude Matters	56
Reaching Out to Others	59
In Her Own Words	63
Decisions	65

Inspiration

Thinking About Inspiration	*69*
The Kosel	*70*
Be an Inspiration	*72*
Determination is Important	*75*
Inspiring Others	*77*
Reflections on Birthdays	*79*
Growing and Changing	*81*
A Box	*85*
Beginning Something New	*87*
Holidays	*89*
Trust Your Inner Voice	*91*
Letting the Sunshine Inside	*94*
A Gift From Above	*95*
Second Chance	*97*
Memorable Encounters	*98*
Pockets	*99*
Understanding Other People's Needs	*100*

Family & Friends

Family

Drop a Pebble in the Water...	*105*
Recipe For Harmony	*107*
Savor the Magic	*110*
Loyalty	*111*
Siblings Are Forever	*113*

Needlepoint	115
Wise Words	120
Bubby, You Are My Sunshine	122
Sharing a Good Deed	127
The First Time	128
A Joyful Heart	131
Memorable Moments	132
A Mother and Daughter Together	134
Delivering Kindness	136
Caring and Sharing	138
Together in Mitzvos	140

Friends

What Is a True Friend?	142
A Special Friend	144
The Perfect Present	145
The Power of a Smile	146
Just Be Yourself	147
Are You an Introvert or an Extrovert?	150
The Opposite of Peer Pressure	153
Encourage Others	156
Finish the Sentence	158
A Friend to Everyone	160
Appreciate Our Differences	162
Forgive One Insult Every Day	164
Together	166

Triumph

What Is an Accomplishment?	*169*
Triumph	*170*
Unsung Heroes	*172*
For Everything a Blessing	*173*
Thinking of Others	*176*
Help and Support Someone	*178*
Difficult Decisions	*179*
Sarah's Story	*183*
Feige's Story	*185*
Shoes	*187*
Overcoming Disappointment	*190*
A Quiet Breakthrough	*192*
I'm Starving	*194*
The Specialness of "Ordinary" Days	*198*
On Overcoming Fear	*200*
Going Forward	*202*
Simple Things I Can Appreciate	*203*

Dear Friend:

Do you remember me? We met a month ago at the orientation for hospital volunteers. I was impressed when I saw you there. I remember your crisply starched yellow blouse. Your earrings and necklace matched and added a perfect accent. Your hair was drawn back in a neat ponytail. Under your carefree smile there was a serious and determined look in your eye.

I had this feeling that you like to formulate lists. From the moment that the alarm clock rings you have many routine tasks to accomplish. I would guess that after the meeting you went home to help with supper, babysit, fix your blow dryer, bring your dress to the cleaners, buy film for your camera and mix salad for your dnner, write back to your pen-pal and read A G.I.F.T. FOR TEENS.

A G.I.F.T. For Teens is a jubilant collection of inspiring words to escort you when you are feeling happy and comforting words to help you when you are feeling down. The book is divided into four sections that cover the topics you want to know more about. The four sections spell out the word G.I.F.T. They are:

>   **G** . . . . Gratitude
>   **I** . . . . Inspiration
>   **F** . . . . Family and Friends
>   **T** . . . . Triumph

There are stories that will make you laugh, conversations to make you think, poems and a whole lot more.

You have dreams and goals. Your routine may include studying, socializing, shopping, and dieting. These things are all important in one way or another but they are incomplete. You want to accomplish something great. You want to make a real difference in your life and in the lives of others. Secretly you wonder — aren't we here on earth to accomplish something more? You feel shy to talk about these things yet you wonder — Are you the only one?

Believe it or not, you are not alone. Many people wonder how they can become the person they want to be. Many of us wish that we could somehow accomplish something wonderful, but somehow we can't find the path to that lofty goal.

This small book overflows with a lot of powerful ideas. Where did these ideas come from? Will they only help strong-willed or talented people to improve, or will they work for ordinary people too? The inspiration and triumph you will find in these pages came directly from girls like you. The "recipes" that are offered here have been tested in the "kitchen" of real life.

The teenagers you will meet in these stories have actually practiced the Torah concepts outlined in the following pages, and they have developed the confidence and strength to improve their lives. They have displayed simple wisdom, self-control, and extraordinary kindness. Some of the teens you will meet in this book had a valid reason to be miserable, and yet they were not. Some were struggling with pain, but they worked hard to overcome obstacles and to give to others. There are girls who go to feed chronically ill patients every week, become a friend to a handicapped child, or decide to befriend a lonely classmate. One group of high school students raised money for an immigrant bride's household needs. Every one of their accomplishments, no matter how small it may have appeared outwardly, was a personal triumph. Each new achievement gave them a sense of pride and the encouragement to go further.

And the best part is that they are all ordinary teenagers, like you. They challenged discouraging attitudes — and so can you.

Rabbi Samson Raphael Hirsch explains that a feeling of progression is synonymous with happiness, because the Hebrew word for happiness — *simchah* — is related to the word *tzemicha*, meaning growth. We do not need to be finished to feel good; we simply need to be on the way.

The teenagers you will meet on these pages will show you how to take small steps toward growth. There are also exercises to do along the way that will give you a feeling of progress. These pages will help you make your wonderful dreams become a reality.

Sincerely,
Roiza Weinreich

Part 1

Gratitude

Gratitude

At the start of the Gratitude section, I'd like to take the opportunity to express my own gratitude to my dear parents. They have made many of my dreams become actualities. Their encouragement, helpfulness and love make every day wonderful. My mother-in-law has encouraged all my various undertakings. The first one to read significant portions of the book was my husband, Faivel. He patiently encouraged me not to give up when I faced minor setbacks.

I would like to thank all my students, too many to mention individually by name, for inspiring me to write this book. Thank you to the teens throughout the United States who contributed, especially to the students of Bais Yaakov High School and Seattle Hebrew Academy. I've learned a lot from all of my students; only some of these lessons are recorded in this book.

I also extend a special note of acknowledgement to Ethel Gottlieb. This is the third book we've written together. I feel that this is our book. Her insight, wisdom and creative ideas added so much to the book you are about to read. Gratitude goes to Rabbis Meir Zlotowitz and Nosson Scherman for their help in bringing about the impressive success of all my books. My special thanks to Rabbi Sheah Brander whose expert knowledge and creativity made the book complete. Rabbi Avrohom Biderman is efficient yet sensitive; my thanks for his insight and helpfulness. My appreciation to the entire ArtScroll staff.

I am filled with gratitude to Hashem for endowing me with the capacity to teach Torah thoughts through writing. I never stop marveling at the far-reaching miracle of each book that was published. My books are here for you, dear readers. I'm glad that I can add a smile to your day. I'd like to express an especially warm thank you to all of the enthusiastic readers around the globe who have written warm letters of encouragement.

Roiza Weinreich

A Gratitude Journal

What is a Gratitude Journal?

Keeping a journal is a great thing to do. A journal is your place to communicate with yourself. When you read past entries you'll see how much you've changed. The things you write make a difference in your life for many reasons. I've kept a journal for six years that I call a Gratitude Journal and it's helped me remember the good things that are happening in my life.

A Gratitude Journal is different because in it you record the good things that happened each day. I don't only write down the good things that happen to me, I write down the good things that happened to others as well. My goal is to write two pages a day.

A Gratitude Journal Can Help You:

Remember Things — I've recorded the day and time that my great-nieces and great-nephews were born. I've written down details about those momentous days. I know that if I hadn't made a note of it when it happened I wouldn't be able to recall it even six months later. Now I can share details with my great-nieces and nephews about the day they were born.

Understand Yourself — Sometimes we forget about our past success when we are in the middle of a problem. A Gratitude Journal helps you remember that Hashem helped you with past worries. This gives you strength. You feel that Hashem will help you in the present as well.

Know Yourself Better — Write down things that are important to you every day. After a while you'll notice a pattern. Looking at what you've written will help you know yourself better.

Like Yourself — Persistence can be a source of pride. The fact that you can decide to write two pages a day and stay with the resolution for several months, a year or a few years is something you can feel proud of.

Guidelines:

- Date every entry.
- A journal entry can be long or short.
- Don't feel bad if you miss a day, but try to make writing down good news a regular habit.

What are you thankful for?

PEOPLE

1. _____
2. _____
3. _____

FAVORITE BOOKS

1. _____
2. _____
3. _____

PLACES YOU'VE VISITED

1. _____
2. _____
3. _____

PROBLEMS THAT WERE RESOLVED

1. _____
2. _____
3. _____

OTHER

1. _____

2. _____

3. _____

How Calm And Content Are You?

HOW FREQUENTLY HAVE YOU:

1. Done a repetitious act patiently (e.g. rewrite, wash dishes)?
   VERY RARELY — 1 ☐ 2 ☐ 3 ☐ 4 ☐ 5 ☐ — VERY FREQUENTLY

2. Noticed how calm and even your pulse is?
   VERY RARELY — 1 ☐ 2 ☐ 3 ☐ 4 ☐ 5 ☐ — VERY FREQUENTLY

3. Accomplished what you set out to do?
   VERY RARELY — 1 ☐ 2 ☐ 3 ☐ 4 ☐ 5 ☐ — VERY FREQUENTLY

4. Accepted your younger sister's foolish mistake?
   VERY RARELY — 1 ☐ 2 ☐ 3 ☐ 4 ☐ 5 ☐ — VERY FREQUENTLY

5. Taken the time to do something that you really enjoy?
   VERY RARELY — 1 ☐ 2 ☐ 3 ☐ 4 ☐ 5 ☐ — VERY FREQUENTLY

6. Waited with patience?
   VERY RARELY — 1 ☐ 2 ☐ 3 ☐ 4 ☐ 5 ☐ — VERY FREQUENTLY

7. Felt cheerful on an ordinary day?
   VERY RARELY — 1 ☐ 2 ☐ 3 ☐ 4 ☐ 5 ☐ — VERY FREQUENTLY

8. Taken several short breaks during the day?
   VERY RARELY — 1 ☐ 2 ☐ 3 ☐ 4 ☐ 5 ☐ — VERY FREQUENTLY

9. Finished a job more quickly than you had expected?
   VERY RARELY — 1 ☐ 2 ☐ 3 ☐ 4 ☐ 5 ☐ — VERY FREQUENTLY

10. Felt calm during a competition even though you were not the best?

   VERY RARELY — 1 ☐ 2 ☐ 3 ☐ 4 ☐ 5 ☐ — VERY FREQUENTLY

11. Volunteered for tasks and responsibilities?

   VERY RARELY — 1 ☐ 2 ☐ 3 ☐ 4 ☐ 5 ☐ — VERY FREQUENTLY

12. Thought that what you do is very important?

   VERY RARELY — 1 ☐ 2 ☐ 3 ☐ 4 ☐ 5 ☐ — VERY FREQUENTLY

13. Moved, walked or eaten at a leisurely pace?

   VERY RARELY — 1 ☐ 2 ☐ 3 ☐ 4 ☐ 5 ☐ — VERY FREQUENTLY

14. Taken time to relax with a schoolmate?

   VERY RARELY — 1 ☐ 2 ☐ 3 ☐ 4 ☐ 5 ☐ — VERY FREQUENTLY

15. Taken time to relax with your mother or other family member?

   VERY RARELY — 1 ☐ 2 ☐ 3 ☐ 4 ☐ 5 ☐ — VERY FREQUENTLY

16. Felt enthusiastic?

   VERY RARELY — 1 ☐ 2 ☐ 3 ☐ 4 ☐ 5 ☐ — VERY FREQUENTLY

17. Handed in a competent though not perfect job and felt you are O.K.?

   VERY RARELY — 1 ☐ 2 ☐ 3 ☐ 4 ☐ 5 ☐ — VERY FREQUENTLY

18. Felt optimistic?

   VERY RARELY — 1 ☐ 2 ☐ 3 ☐ 4 ☐ 5 ☐ — VERY FREQUENTLY

19. Felt encouraged?

   VERY RARELY — 1 ☐ 2 ☐ 3 ☐ 4 ☐ 5 ☐ — VERY FREQUENTLY

20. Laughed at a joke?

   VERY RARELY — 1 ☐ 2 ☐ 3 ☐ 4 ☐ 5 ☐ — VERY FREQUENTLY

21. Held yourself back from talking about people who disappointed you?

   VERY RARELY — 1 ☐ 2 ☐ 3 ☐ 4 ☐ 5 ☐ — VERY FREQUENTLY

22. Found your papers, notebooks and folders right away?
   VERY RARELY — 1 ☐ 2 ☐ 3 ☐ 4 ☐ 5 ☐ — VERY FREQUENTLY

23. Fallen asleep easily and slept well?
   VERY RARELY — 1 ☐ 2 ☐ 3 ☐ 4 ☐ 5 ☐ — VERY FREQUENTLY

24. Felt appreciated?
   VERY RARELY — 1 ☐ 2 ☐ 3 ☐ 4 ☐ 5 ☐ — VERY FREQUENTLY

25. Found it easy to slow down?
   VERY RARELY — 1 ☐ 2 ☐ 3 ☐ 4 ☐ 5 ☐ — VERY FREQUENTLY

26. Felt satisfied with what you had?
   VERY RARELY — 1 ☐ 2 ☐ 3 ☐ 4 ☐ 5 ☐ — VERY FREQUENTLY

The rating for this test isn't important. There is no mark, because the main goal here is to learn and grow. You may use this quiz on an occasional basis as a barometer for yourself and others. You can also read it in the beginning of the day to get a clearer view of your goals. This self-test helps you ask yourself, "What do I spend my time thinking about? Are my thoughts helpful and positive or not?" Each of these questions can become a new pair of glasses that you can try on and use to view the world from a positive perspective. This volume will show you how to do this in greater detail.

Getting Started

You don't have to buy a small diary with a lock and a tiny space for each day. A scrap book, blank book or three-ring loose-leaf binder will give you more space to be creative. In school you've probably kept a journal in a small spiral notebook. This kind of journal is easy to take around with you. You can write in it almost anywhere.

Your journal doesn't have to be black and white. There are many supplies you can use to make it more exciting:

Scissors — Cut out beautiful pictures from wrapping paper, catalogs and magazines. Sometimes there are photographs that aren't perfect. Save them and create a collage.

Glue – Glue sticks work very well because they aren't messy and drippy.

Stickers – Stickers are fun! They make your journal fun to write in and fun to read. Stickers can make your journal festive. They put you in the mood to celebrate.

Markers – Fine line markers work best. You don't have to be an artist to make a creative border or add dots of color that match your stickers. You can decorate your page according to a specific theme around your stickers.

Tape – You might want to tape a poem or saying into your journal.

Pens – I collect pens of different colors so that I can make my entries stand out.

These are the basics. I'm sure you'll have many other good ideas.

Enjoy This Moment

Enjoy this moment!
As changes unfold
Accept them—
Your life is directed from Above
So, relax.

Enjoy this moment!
Remember that your life
Is a sacred journey.
You are in a custom-made
Time and place—
Everything that transpires
Was precisely planned.

Enjoy this moment!
You are in this precise place
At this exact time only once—
You won't be exactly here again.

Enjoy this moment!
You can touch serenity
At this time
By doing your best.

Enjoy this moment!
Say the right words,
Do the right thing,
Be your own friend.
This moment revolves around you!

The Gratitude State

Direct experience of gratitude happens in many ways. It is something we all have at one time or another, but may not have recognized. I call this experience the "gratitude state." When you enter the gratitude state you feel close to Hashem and you feel Hashem is watching over you. You may be unaware of the change in yourself, but others often notice. They see it in your face and hear it in your voice.

•❖ *Trees*

The tree towers above me. It has five straight branches that reach up so high. I feel that they might touch the heavens. There is dark green and clay green moss on one side of the tree. Every three feet there is a knot on the trunk. A tiny spider crept down from the tree and wandered onto the page. The green leaves aren't identical; each leaf has a slightly different curve. A breeze enters and makes the branches sway gently. The thin branches sink under the weight of the leaves. I see the sun shining down between the branches. It's brilliant and white like a star.

A fly buzzes past my ear. A bird sings and calls to his comrades. The rustle, the crickets and the birds calling are the only sounds I hear. The shade of this tree is pleasant. It's 101 degrees today but I can sit here under the shelter of this ancient tree and enjoy a breeze humming in my ears. I feel peaceful, comfortable and protected under the leafy canopy.

I want to sit here and wonder. I want to forget the concerns that I left at the bottom of the hill and stay up here on the top of the hill.

I want to count the branches and the leaves. I'll sit here and observe spiders and wild mushrooms, ferns, branches and leaves.

Right now I don't want to look at a clock or answer a telephone. I want to sit with my back to the road and ignore the sound of speeding cars. I want to fully enter a majestic, silent world.

The breeze dances around my shoulders. The birds sing. Their song changes with each moment. The bark of the tree feels rough in some places and smooth in others. Imagine! I've come up this hill daily for many years but I've always rushed past this beautiful spot. It was waiting calmly for me to enter for 100 years.

The breeze is blowing stronger now. I could sit here for another pleasant hour. Well, this peaceful glen will continue to wait patiently for me to visit again.

I don't doubt that you would love to visit this peaceful spot right now. However, you may be far away from a forest when you read this. Just because you can't surround yourself with trees today or tomorrow doesn't mean you can't appreciate the beauty of Hashem's creations. When we notice Hashem's creations we feel closer to Him and it affects our outlook on life. Every day we pass something beautiful without pausing to notice.

•← How Sunshine Makes Me Glad

It was a typical rainy Seattle day in the middle of February. The cold, wet weather made me feel gloomy—especially on my Shabbat birthday. On top of the gloomy weather, I was upset because I couldn't find the dress I wanted to wear, my brother was picking on me and I was having a bad hair day. Then I left for the synagogue with my mother. As we approached the synagogue, I felt a glow coming from behind me. I turned around and saw the beautiful sun shining. The sun brightened the day. I knew at that moment that I was going to have a bright Shabbat birthday after all.

Miriam Siscovick

Sometimes when I'm feeling sad, I notice the sun break through the gloomy clouds. It makes me warm and happy and helps me forget the sad thought. The sun makes me feel daring and adventurous. It gives me the urge to share with everyone.

I wish that the sun would be out everyday. Actually there is a sunny part within us that we all share. If you listen to your heart, you will find sunshine there. So today, I pray, if I may, that the sun rise in the sky and in my heart too. Let us be happy in every way!

Jennifer Miller

༄༅

In the fall we step on colorful leaves without bending to pick them up. It was only when we were five or six that we collected them and made them into a collage. Now, we have outgrown that. In the winter someone will call out that it's snowing and we may not even run to the window to take a peek. Did we notice the first crocus blooming this past spring? We are too busy so we defer entering the gratitude state. Let's stop denying ourselves this uncomplicated pleasure!

Hashem Will Take Care Of You!

Who is the Neshama living within? Why is it trapped inside? Why are we too busy to notice our good fortune, benefits and conveniences? We look for something more to bring us happiness when we can be happy **immediately**. Enjoy your good fortune right now. Enjoy the present—it's a gift.

❧❧❧

QUESTION: *What incident has left an impact on your life?*

J.M.: I was in an auto accident a few years ago.

QUESTION: *What happened to you after the accident?*

J.M.: As soon as I hit my head I felt my skin stretch and a bump formed. Hatzolah—the volunteer ambulance—was called and they checked my vital signs. As the days went on the swelling went down, but my eyes had blue circles around them. I wore sunglasses for a while.

QUESTION: *What were your thoughts when it happened?*

J.M.: I felt like I was on a roller coaster. In fact, since then I won't ride on a roller coaster. I was being spun around by the impact of the crash. I noticed, though, that while I was being spun around, the rest of the world still went on. Nothing stops.

QUESTION: *What was your first thought after the accident?*

J.M.: I remember staring at the trees above and thinking—I must be alive. I wouldn't be able to see the trees if I *chas v'shalom* wouldn't be living.

QUESTION: *Have you learned anything from this experience?*

J.M.: I learned not to rush. Every moment counts. Enjoy life and don't become nervous.

QUESTION: *How have you resolved to change?*

J.M.: I try not to become stressed out. I try to do things calmly and I don't get nervous over trivial problems. Take each day as it comes. Hashem is always there with you.

I learned a very important lesson from J.M. She takes each day in stride. We must appreciate what we have. Before we know it we'll be older and we'll regret not having taken the time to appreciate what was there for us. Hashem is always with us in every aspect of our life. Relax!

Hashem will take care of all your needs!

Wake Up And See

While you are waiting for happiness to find you, happiness is waiting for you to find it.

Don't wait for gratitude to find you. Create a beautiful garden in which your gratitude can flourish.

Commit yourself completely and wholeheartedly to collecting grateful thoughts.

The power of your commitment will nourish the seeds of your gratitude. The ordinary blessings that occur at each moment of life will blossom in your heart and give you a feeling of satisfaction.

Racheli said, "Life is a gift given to us by God. The gift is limited. There is an hourglass and the sands of time slowly slide by, moment by moment. We don't know how many grains are allotted to us. Let us caress each one we have before it slips away. We can't catch and hold each grain of time. Yet we can savor each one's texture and size as it slips out of our grasp."

We wake up each morning and open our eyes, but do we really see? We take our vision for granted. We should appreciate every function that our body faithfully performs. One who survives a major accident realizes this. We should not need a catastrophe to enable us to enjoy our vision.

Little incidents can make you aware of bigger things. When I went to the eye doctor, he inserted some drops. The drops obscured my vision. The doctor told me to keep my eyes shut for ten minutes. Those ten minutes of blindness made me aware of the darkness that a blind person experiences.

During those long minutes I realized with astonishing clarity how much we have to be grateful for.

Chaya L.

It was the end of a hectic Friday afternoon. My mother was lighting the Shabbos candles. At the time, I was an 18-month-old baby cheerfully crawling on the floor. I got up, using the door to my brother's room to support myself. He closed the door—he hadn't realized that I was there. The door slammed on my finger, causing it to fall off. My mother ran to the phone to call the ambulance. I spent that Friday night in the emergency room. The doctors weren't sure that they could reattach my finger. Thank God after undergoing surgery, stitches and a cast, my finger looks almost normal. This certainly helped me appreciate my fingers.

Tova G.

Mother

When I read this chapter to a colleague she said, "It brings tears to my eyes." I wasn't feeling especially jubilant or inspired when I wrote it. One might think that compelling writing can only be generated when the mood strikes. However, sometimes it's best to ignore the voice that says, "You can't," and instead, jump in and try to create a meaningful thought. I began and so it has become. Afterwards, I felt jubilant.

~~~

When good feelings are shared, they double. To master the art of doing this and to create a microcosm of serenity and security for those we love may take planning. How and where do we begin?

I call my mother every morning at 8:30. It's good to know that someone really wants to hear about the good things that are happening to me and that their contentment will increase. Before the call I prepare. I think of something good that happened within the family. I decide on an adorable anecdote or an example of the children's activities that I want to share. I may recall that a child shared or was considerate. If I recently received my children's report cards, I'll read some of their better grades. Today when I called, my mother surprised me.

The phone rang five times and my mother picked up. "Good morning," I said.

My mother answered, "Mazal Tov."

"Mommy, tell me the good news."

"I'm leaving for a *bris* right now. One of your cousins had a grandson." For a moment I felt like dropping everything and going too. What would all the children do, however, if I disappeared at 8 A.M.?

My mother's cheerful "Mazel Tov" echoes in my ears. It's a glorious way to begin a day. I visualize her smile. I can see her standing at the door all dressed up in her Shabbos dress with her face made up, ready to go to the celebration. I'm so delighted that my parents are well and can be busy going and rejoicing. I know that the grandmother will be overjoyed to see my parents there. I laugh quietly with delight.

I pray too: May I always hear good news when I call those I love. May I begin many days with "Mazal Tov."

Food Is A Delight

This section allows you to experience, through various humorous and thought provoking descriptions, a deeper perspective on the food we eat. In different ways, you will appreciate that food is precious. While each entry can be read separately, they complement each other.

People have many feelings about food. If you were to ask most people, "How was lunch?" you'd probably hear something like, "It was O.K., I guess." Many people feel that food is simply okay. Even those who report having a good relationship with food express irritation and frustration at times. What they may not realize is that our gratitude for the food we eat can grow with a little extra effort. Gratitude as we savor our food will help us enjoy life. Perhaps one of these excerpts will help you experience your next meal more completely.

Most people overlook the miraculous ways that food grows. You know that tomatoes and raspberries don't grow on supermarket shelves. Cucumbers and radishes don't magically appear on your plate. Rivky and Chana Malya discovered that every vegetable and fruit is a wonder. Are you ready to appreciate and enjoy your vegetables as they do?

◦❖ *The Garden*

On visits to my grandmother as a young girl, I would hold her wrinkled hand as we explored her vegetable garden. I was enclosed in a green wonderland. I plucked red tomatoes from vines that were taller than I was. Ripe raspberries seemed to fall off their stems at my finger's command. Green beans and peas inched up chicken wire fences. I grabbed them before they would climb out of reach. Two green leaves peeking out of the earth caught my attention. I pulled and was astonished to see a dirty red radish hanging on. On the way back, my hands were full so I couldn't hold my grandmother's hand. Instead, she placed her wrinkled hand on my shoulder and led me back to her house.

Rivky B.

❧ A Day On The Farm

*B*right and early one Sunday morning, an overloaded car full of eager, anticipating children pulled into the farm's spacious parking lot. Miles of land filled to capacity with many varieties of luscious fruits and fresh vegetables stood before our eyes. Never had we seen so many eggplants in one spot, some fully grown, others just beginning to ripen into a rich purple color. I had never known that zucchini have pretty flowers. Here we recognized the wonders of creation. An Artist gave each and every fruit and vegetable its own unique qualities.

Chana Malya K.

Gratitude. It's more powerful than any other ingredient in the happiness formula. Some people want to be happy very badly. They get up every morning and go to bed every night dreaming of happiness. Yet they can be happy right now by seeing how the ordinary things they enjoy every day are actually wonderful.

❧ Rain's Vital Blessing

Everyone grows up with characteristic sayings that their parents repeated often to them. These sayings are absorbed in our self-conscious many years before we can comprehend their deeper meaning. As we grow older we begin to think about and apply these messages. They remind us of the precious qualities of our parents that we want to treasure and emulate.

I remember my parents talking about the rain when I was a little girl. Their thinking was very optimistic. We were once sitting around the tiny table in the kitchen, and my mother hurried to close the shutters because a storm had erupted. She stood looking out at the lightning, thunder and rain and said, "Thank G-d we have a roof over our heads. When we were running from city to city, only one step ahead of the Nazis *Yemach Shemam*, there was no shelter from the rain. You just had to continue running."

My father glanced outside and said philosophically, "Rain in itself is also good. If it wouldn't rain, you wouldn't have what to eat."

Tehillim speaks of this wonderful process: **"He waters the mountains from the treasury in the Heavens; from the fruit of the clouds the earth's thirst is quenched."** ***Borchi Nafshi* (104:13)**.

The most vital blessing that comes down with the rain is food. The wheat that eventually becomes flour and bread, the grass eaten by the cows, who in turn provide us with milk and meat (not together of course), and the 260 different types of fruits and vegetables available in the average supermarket all grow because it rained.

We take the rain and our food for granted and remain discontented because our minds are busy with our other problems, but each meal could be elevated into a ceremony of service to Hashem if we took the time to properly appreciate the food and its source. The sages instructed us to make a blessing over rain three times a day and over each food, so that we should appreciate this important relationship.

◆❖ *The Painting On The Wall*

*T*here is an interesting painting on the wall in my parents' dining room. On a bare wood table there is half a small loaf of old, dry bread, with a knife near it, a large slice of watermelon, two young onions and a clay jug. It's not a very pretty picture though it was well done and the food looks real. I always wondered about it and one day I asked my father, "Why is this painting in the dining room?"

He answered,

"When I lived in Russia, in Samarkand during World War II, every day of life was a gift. There were many times that I was hungry and I wasn't sure if I would pull through. That painting represents a big meal in Samarkand. If you had that much food to eat at one time you felt like making a party.

"When I sit at the Shabbos table each week, I'm surrounded by your mother and your sister and brother. Your mother brings out one delicious dish after another and we are comfortable and we have peace and the silver candlesticks and the silver becher on the white tablecloth smile to me. I try not to take a single bite for granted. Each week I thank Hashem that He rescued me from there and brought me here."

Each time my father says a berachah in a loud, clear voice and he glances at the painting, he is nourished by the attitude that rain, food, peace, health, family and all the other blessings he enjoys are a gift from Hashem.

Practice this attitude before you say a berachah. Are you holding a delicious golden peach in your hand? Think about the wind and the rain that nourished the peach tree and helped it grow. Think about all the forces that Hashem watched over and coordinated to bring that peach to you. You will learn not only to have a different response to rain, but you will be in a better mood all the time.

When one supplements his meals with gratitude, the results are remarkable. Remember that each raindrop brings a present *for you from Hashem. Review the evidence of the benefits of rain and you can enhance the quality of your life. As the Rebbe of Kobrin zt"l says, "You are where your thoughts are."*

"Every person should search in his situation for the kindness of Hashem. The main ingredient in man is his power of thought. We are where our thoughts are. If a person proceeds in his life with the thought that Hashem is kind to him and finds Hashem's kindness in every occurrence he draws Hashem's blessing upon him. If he does the opposite and thinks that Hashem is judging him and therefore complains and is upset he draws Hashem's judgments upon him."

(Concepts in Chasidus: *Rebbe of Kobrin*, pg. 70)

Bread

Puah Shteiner was a seven-year-old child during the difficult period of Israel's War of Independence in 1948. She describes her experiences when The Old City was under siege and there were shortages of bread and water.

It was Wednesday afternoon. We children were sitting inside the small cells of the storeroom, the adults were outside in the passageways. Despair was in their eyes. In addition to everything else, there was now no more bread. We weren't yet hungry, but a few hours later, our stomachs began to rumble. Soon we were lethargic. None of the adults said a word. Only the children demanded, "Bread! We want bread!"

Of the whole group, only two men stood up: the head of the Eizen family, his blonde beard and sidelocks white with dust and... Abba, who had unceasingly and uncomplainingly carried the heavy burden of the community on his shoulders since the start of the war.

"We will go to the bakery," the two men announced.

Silence fell on the storeroom, and in the silence, the two turned to go out.

"No! No!" screamed Naomi. But Abba and Binyamin Eizen were already gone.

People cried silently. Would the men succeed in reaching the bakery? Would they return safely?

The shrinking Jewish Quarter was being bombarded heavily but my sister Naomi almost overwhelmed the noise of the gunfire destroying our homes and streets. We had no idea whether the Arabs had captured the bakery yet or not. My heart felt like a shell about to explode.

"Abba, Abba, why did they let you go? Why you? There are other people here who could go! I'm not hungry, Abba! I don't want any bread. I only want you ... you, safe and sound."

Each moment Abba was gone seemed like an eternity. The

shells continued to fly. When would Abba return?

"Please, God, protect him!" I cried from the bottom of my heart.

Shouts and cries of joy suddenly filled the dark passageway. They were here! They had returned! Thank God! Just at that moment, a shell exploded in the courtyard nearby.

Everyone ran out to the passageway, jumping on the two men, each of whom carried a huge sack on his back. The fragrant smell of fresh pita bread filled the air, causing our mouths to water. The two men were surrounded and almost trampled.

"Stand in line!" shouted Abba in an attempt to discipline the hungry crowd. "No one will get so much as a crumb if he doesn't stand in line," shouted Abba again, closing his hands tightly around the mouth of the sack.

Slowly the people formed a line. Abba took out two pitot and handed them to the first person in line. Another two... and another two... The sack was rapidly being emptied, and there was still a long line of people. Dozens of hands reached towards every pita as it emerged from the sack. Abba shouted again, "There is enough for everyone," but the people were too panic-stricken to pay heed. Everyone knew that no one would risk his life again to go to the bakery and bake. In another hour or two, the bakery, complete with its stock of flour, would probably be in Arab hands.

Abba continued to distribute pitot. Each one was grabbed up the minute it emerged from the sack. No one wanted to miss out on his last piece of bread. The sacks were almost empty. Imma, who had not pushed forward until then, tried to get through to Abba.

"You haven't given me any yet!" she called in a choking voice, "Give me, too! Your own children are hungry!" She waved her hands until Abba noticed her.

"After everyone else has received, we too will receive ours." Abba continued distributing pitot to the crowd.

Finally, the pressure lessened. Imma, too, received two pitot *(no more!), and took us back to the musty cell. Each of us received a piece of pita, over which we recited the blessing for bread. The little ones ate heartily, but as for me, the fresh pita stuck in my throat. It was hard to swallow bread for which my father had risked his life.*

(Forever My Jerusalem, *Puah Shteiner pg. 128*)

Honoring Hashem

1. How can I show that I love Hashem?
2. Are my ordinary actions important?
3. How can I make the ideals I learn a reality?

As you look at these three questions—and the answers you get when answering them—you can see that you are closer to the principles you've learned about than you had previously thought.

Honoring Hashem can be accomplished in many practical ways.

Look further. You can use your resourcefulness to make each Shabbos meal unique. The holiness of the day is enhanced by your creativity. When you make something beautiful and delicious to honor Shabbos, you enjoy the results immediately. When people are productive, happy and get along, they are also honoring Hashem.

Every celebration is enhanced by beautiful food. Fruits and vegetables lend color and beauty to the banquet table.

There you are. You stand and admire the platters. The shapes and colors are tastefully arranged to accentuate the natural, delicious beauty of each fruit and vegetable.

You enjoy it even more when you contemplate the loving effort that was invested to create these extremely positive results. The completed banquet table is more precious when you had a part in the preparations.

In camp one Motzai Shabbos, a group of girls gathered in the kitchen to cut up fruit for Melava Malkah. While one girl peeled the orange cantaloupe, another peeled sweet, ripe honeydew. In the meantime, a third girl sliced the red watermelon. Each girl worked with a different fruit, but they had a common goal. Their goal was to prepare the fruits and arrange them on platters. The finished product was an elegant array of beautiful colors that took my breath away.

Tova L.

A Bottle Of Wine

There are periods that motivate a person to do something unique. This certainly applies to fulfilling mitzvos that are related to food. The joy and spirit of Purim filled me with exciting ideas. Everyone sends their closest relatives and friends a food basket and a bottle of wine. My plan was to do something special. Not only would I dress up, but my wine bottle would have a costume too!

With scraps of fabric, ribbon and pieces of an old wig I created the costume. I made a long black satin coat to wrap around the base of the bottle. I placed white felt on the front of the bottle. I drew a shirt and short breeches and socks on the felt. The shoes were attached separately for a three dimensional effect. I made the face with peach colored lining and added a beard of authentic hair cut from the old wig. The *peyos* hung down from the *shtreimel*. My tall Chassid stood proudly. He looked perfect.

My *chason* and his family all smiled and laughed when they received my unique *Mishloach Manos* accompanied by the Chasid wine bottle doll. They put the wine bottle doll in a place of honor in the breakfront. I saw it every Shabbos for several years when I visited. It stood guard and smiled out of the breakfront window.

Once a niece came to visit. She insisted on playing with the enchanting Chassid doll in the breakfront. She was a child who got her requests. No one could predict or prevent what happened next.

The bottle was heavy and the glue had weakened with age. When this niece picked up the doll by the head the top suddenly came off. The bottle slipped down, hitting her toes.

My niece began crying. She was so excited she couldn't even decide which toe was bruised. My husband got her to calm down. He put ten band aids on her toes to cover all the possibilities.

The bottle didn't break and on the next Shabbos we had a *L'chaim*.

Beyond Marble Cake

Marble cake is an everyday, all-the-time thing. Marble cake is more unassuming than other cakes. One usually doesn't get excited about marble cake. At a party you choose the marble cake if you are on a diet and are looking for something simple. Yet Esty learned two important ideas from her first attempt at making marble cake from scratch — to appreciate marble cake intensely and to persist in achieving her goals despite unexpected difficulties.

> *Did you know that the humble marble cake is actually a complicated food? Last week I began what I thought would be an easy task of baking a cake. First I had to separate the eggs. I had never done it before. As if that wasn't enough, the book also instructed me to mix the cocoa and vanilla batters separately. As I bravely continued to add ingredients, another item in the book caught my attention: "Pour each batter separately into the pan." I panicked! Now even pouring the batter had become a major task. I fearfully slipped my interesting batter into the oven and retrieved it an hour later. My effort had succeeded; however, it had not been a picnic.*

The next time you eat something as simple as marble cake, consider its real value. It's true that we tend to simply bite in without focusing on an important truth — food is precious. Thinking about the many details that had to be coordinated to bring you your morning breakfast can help you appreciate its value. Where did the sugar for your hot cocoa come from? Where did the wheat for your bread or marble cake grow? In which country did the cocoa beans grow? How were they processed?

Not one day goes by that we don't think about our dreams and goals. We think about how great it would be to try something new, conquer a bad habit, or reach out to someone in need. Obstacles, however, are frightful things. When we encounter difficulties we often give up.

How would Esty's cake turn out if she skipped some of the ingredients? What happens to a cake when one puts in a little extra flour and two eggs less than the recipe calls for? Would the cake have a marble design if one didn't pour the batters separately? We have often seen the results of taking a shortcut. It's not very pretty or tasty. However, Esty's experience doesn't apply only to baking.

Don't pass over this anecdote lightly. We're talking here about something that can help you change your life. I know this idea works. If you're serious about doing something special with your life, it's important to persist, even when things become more difficult than you expected them to be. When Hashem sees we really want to accomplish a goal, He helps us in ways we never anticipated.

You can't succeed overnight. It might take days or weeks, but how badly do you want to succeed?

The Secret Ingredient

Everyone looks for ways to enjoy life. Food can be a treat that helps us feel better. When we indulge once too often, food can make us feel full of remorse. We can enjoy the way food looks and tastes, but we can also enjoy food on a deeper level.

After you try to bake a cake on your own you begin to appreciate all the cakes your mother has served. You may have been eating a certain cake for years yet have never delighted in it until you tried to make it. Those cakes didn't magically appear. Somehow when you take a slice of the first cake you've successfully created the texture is lighter, the cake looks more inviting, the chocolate is sweeter and the icing is creamier.

Food helps us celebrate. We eat challah on Shabbos, latkes on Chanuka, blintzes on Shavuos, hamantashen on Purim and honey cake on Rosh Hashanah. Food brings back memories as well.

Many ingredients go into our food. Along with the eggs, flour, oil and cocoa, there are ingredients that make the cake taste good. Sugar and vanilla are added to the batter as well. In addition, there is a secret ingredient that goes into the homemade food we enjoy. That ingredient is the love of the person who prepared it for us.

When we remember the love that's in the food, the ordinary becomes extraordinary. It's not just a piece of cake, it's a tradition. It's not just a food that's eaten every year, it's a link between the generations. Estee and Bashy discovered that honey cake and challah can have a deep significance.

> *During one of my family's annual erev Rosh Hashanah visits to my grandparents' home, my grandmother was in the process of making honey cake. She bustled around the kitchen, taking out ingredients, cracking and checking eggs, measuring flour and pouring oil. When she saw me, her face lit up with joy and pride. "My child, watch as I make the cake so one day you can bake it for your grandchildren," my grandmother said. This year's honey cake tasted different. Each slice*

possessed the love and care of my grandmother who worked and toiled to make it for us.

Estee B.

✿ Challah

As I walked into my house I saw my mother baking challah. She started by putting all the ingredients into the machine. After ten minutes she had a thick dough. She took it out of the bowl and placed it in a warm spot to rise. The dough was separated into pieces and rolled into long ropes. My mother makes braiding the challah look simple. The golden egg and sesame seeds went on top as a final touch. The challah was placed in the oven. A few minutes later we were able to smell the heavenly aroma that rose out of the oven. The challos looked crispy and brown when they came out of the oven. They tasted like heaven.

Bashy G.

Thorns Have Roses!

Some People Are Always Complaining
That Roses Have Thorns,
I'm Forever Grateful
That Thorns Have Roses

Alphonse Karr

Thorns do have roses. There are good things happening in your life. There are even good aspects to some of your problems. Work on finding balance. There may be only one rose hiding behind many thorns. You may get scratched trying to push aside the thorns to find the rose. Don't give up. Find the rose. It's worth the struggle. You will find hope, peace of mind and strength if you persist in looking for the rose.

Do you take the one thing you don't have and magnify it? Do you feel inside like you have swallowed a wound up spring? Everyone's life has problems. When we dwell on those problems we force ourselves to run up the down escalator. We expend too much energy chewing over our problems. When the problem is resolved or no longer applies, we can't rest because now there are new problems.

At a *Tehillim* workshop, Necha described someone who looks for the thorns instead of the roses. "I know someone who always has a problem. First she had to decide which high school to attend. When she began high school she worried about having friends. She found one friend but then worried about other girls who were competing for her friend's attention. Don't take the one thing you don't have and magnify it."

Have you ever wondered who decides who will be content; who will have the things they want most; who will have something to smile about each day? Do you think it's the same person who decides who will live uneventful, discouraging lives and who will never have the material things that will give them satisfaction? The answer to these questions is that Hashem has given you the choice.

You are responsible for your happiness now and for the person you will become. Every day you can choose to look for the thorns or to look for the rose.

What happens when someone looks for the rose in her life? A cheerful face lights up a room. A compliment gives a renewed spark of energy. Awareness of the strengths of others rather than their faults helps happiness sprout. Looking for the rose makes one calm and relaxed. One feels happy inside about what they are doing. A positive attitude is the structure that supports every endeavor and sustains us in every hour.

∽∾

When I was a high school student I visited my great aunt and uncle *z"l* every Sunday. Once when I entered I commented, "Aunt Rivka, you look so cheerful this morning. Did anything special happen?" My aunt set the gleaming sugar bowl down near the roses in the crystal vase and said, "Everything is the same as it was yesterday. Your uncle is still ill and I still have dizzy spells. Today, however, I feel better about it. I feel more hopeful. Let me tell you a story that my father used to tell." (Her father was the *Admor* of Bobov, Rav Ben Zion Halberstam, *zt"l*, may his blood be avenged.)

> *There was a water carrier in the Baal Shem Tov's town. The Baal Shem Tov greeted him one morning and asked, "How is everything?"*
>
> *"Absolutely terrible," the water carrier griped. "I'm an old, weak man. This work is much too strenuous. There is no one helping me. When I have to climb many stairs with these heavy buckets the women complain that some water spilled on the steps. Life is miserable."*
>
> *The Baal Shem Tov comforted the man and blessed him but his concern continued. A few weeks later he met the water carrier and asked him, "Have things improved?"*
>
> *"Thank Hashem," the water carrier beamed. "I am so fortunate. I may be old but I am healthy. I can afford the basics and I*

am not a burden on my children. I can help others. When I bring the water, people are grateful. Sometimes they serve me tea."

The Baal Shem Tov explained the water carrier's conflicting responses. Sometimes our situation doesn't change from one day to the next. However, Hashem puts feelings of joy and hope in our hearts. That change of attitude changes our existence.

Some people wake up in the morning and think about their problems. They grumble and mumble the *Modeh Ani* prayer without even realizing that they just said — THANK YOU. Stop for a minute and smile before you say the *Modeh Ani* prayer and remember that you have just received the gift of life.

Expressing gratitude for the miracles that you enjoy every day is the best way to make each moment special. When you first open your eyes in the morning, decide to smile and look for a rose. As your head is still on the pillow, smile and look for something good. Begin your day with a cheerful, sincere Thank You! Don't mumble the words of *Modeh Ani* — sing them! (Sing quietly, not too loud.) Thank you, because right now there is good in my life. Thank you for the good I can do today. Thank you for all the spoonfuls of sweetness I can experience today.

TRY IT!

What Do You Do When Things Go Wrong?

On one of his lecture tapes, Rabbi Avigdor Miller explains, "There are two types of success. When things go smoothly, you have succeeded the easy way. But if you can behave gracefully when things have gone wrong, you have truly succeeded."

When people cooperate and are pleasant and considerate; when you are growing and accomplishing; when you receive the ultimate blessing of being appreciated by your beneficiaries — that is the easy success.

When people are late, but you keep calm; when something you treasure is lost or broken but you don't scream; when you are insulted and you don't answer back — that is true success.

Kaila is a master at staying on course and keeping her perspective when things go wrong. At work I've never seen her speak with impatience to an inept assistant, and when I call her at home she manages to handle numerous interruptions without losing her composure. Several years ago we had to enter the shul to set up for a tzedokah function, but when we arrived at the door with all the food we realized that the key didn't work. Everyone was tense and edgy but Kaila kept calm. She saved the day when she thought of asking a neighbor for help. The neighbor opened the door for us.

I decided to ask Kaila for her ideas on dealing with the problems in our day-to-day existence.

QUESTION: *When did you face a problem that worried you a lot in the past five years?*

KAILA: When we bought our home we had many unexpected expenses. We did repairs in the house and they cost us about twenty percent more than expected. We had to dip into our savings a few times to cover the bills. About a week before the moving date I realized that we didn't have enough money in the bank to pay the movers.

QUESTION: *So you needed to get several hundred dollars in a week's time. What options did you have for getting the money you needed?*

KAILA: We could have asked my parents or in-laws for the money. However, there were problems with that option. I didn't feel comfortable explaining to them how tight we actually were. They probably would have reproached us for spending more than we could afford and getting into this mess. I felt so embarrassed that I asked my husband to do the borrowing.

QUESTION: *I guess you felt that although it wasn't ideal to borrow, you didn't have another choice. Is that how you solved the problem?*

KAILA: Actually, we never did borrow the money. On the night before our move I realized that neither my parents or in-laws had spoken to me about overspending so I concluded that my husband hadn't followed my suggestion. I said, "The movers are coming tomorrow morning. Now it's too late to borrow. How will we pay them?" My husband said, "Don't worry."

QUESTION: *How did you feel? Did you worry?*

KAILA: Of course I worried. I've always taken my responsibilities seriously. My husband's a dentist and we've always met our bills. I felt very uneasy having people come and not having the money for them. My husband was amazing. He was really calm. The next morning when the movers came I whispered to him, "The movers are here. How will we pay?" He answered, "Hashem will help, don't worry." I got really involved in supervising the move after that and I couldn't think of anything else for several hours. Finally the movers finished unloading the truckload of furniture and appliances in our new home. My husband walked over to them with a smile and handed them the full $900.00 in cash.

QUESTION: *You must have been surprised.*

KAILA: I sure was. I was so surprised and elated that I did not even think of asking how he got the money. My husband smiled at me after the movers left and said, "Well, don't you want to know where I got the money? A check came from the I.R.S. in today's mail. It was almost to the penny what we needed. When I cashed the check I had $6.00 change. I told you that Hashem would help us."

QUESTION: *What did you learn from this?*

KAILA: I have quoted this story to my children so many times when we've had problems both minor and major that it is a family classic. Hashem is helping all of us all the time. These minor miracles frequently happen for those who trust in Hashem. Because of their trust they notice Hashem's guidance while others are too busy complaining to see how the Creator provides.

◆ *Someone I Admire*

I was so mad! Thursday is one on my favorite days of the whole week and it was completely wrecked. I was going to go shopping with my mother and now I couldn't because her old car broke down. My mom and I trudged inside, leaving the immobile car outside with the bright red hood wide open.

Our lovely neighbor was driving by and saw that our car hood was wide open. He parked and walked up to the front door to inquire about the irregular state our car was in. "I saw your car hood was open and I was wondering if everything is all right?" he asked.

Mother thanked him and told him what was wrong. From inside the house, I watched him roll up his sleeves, twist this and tighten that under the car's hood. My mom jumped in the car turned the key and the engine started! Mom called to me, "Come on Annike, we're going shopping." I was so delighted.

It was nice of my neighbor to put his life on pause and help us. When he did that he made me want to go out and do kind things for other people and make them just as happy as I was now.

Annike S. Fox

Coping During a Crisis

Someone who can discern the benefit of a difficult situation possesses a vital skill. In all aspects of life it's helpful. Don't expect to smile or shout a cheer during a difficult moment. Rather pause, reflect and accept the overall situation.

When you look for the good, it helps you access harmony every day. You go forward and pass over obstacles and problems. Many challenges that would be overwhelming are seen for what they are. Instead of feeling helpless, you focus on what needs to be done.

After a lot of effort is invested, it's easy to feel disappointed when your day doesn't develop as you had hoped. How will you handle your feeling of failure? How will you find the courage to try again? How will you know what to say to your friends? Elka Rochel found that it helps to redefine success.

> "*We were playing a game of punch ball. We felt excited as the points added up. However, the other team did even better and we lost. Some people on the team felt bad. They thought that the afternoon was a flop because they lost despite their hard work.*
>
> *"There were others who told themselves, 'We achieved because we played well.' If you try and the scoreboard says you lost, don't be discouraged because there is another scoreboard that says you won."*

Strike a balance. We need to look at things from a deeper perspective, but at the same time it's normal to have strong feelings. There are ways to feel grateful even when we feel like a flop. Remember that you did your best and the closeness of your friends is your most important treasure. It's O.K. to plan an occasional treat to lift your mood. Although you would have celebrated your victory, you can still celebrate your friendship.

Harmony

We have spoken about developing appreciation for the "small things" in life, and we've tapped the topic of finding the benefit of a difficult situation. But there is still one more area in which a good attitude can actually save the world: the way in which we cope with things that frighten us.

Do you look at problems as though they were big mountains that you can never climb? Do you feel overwhelmed when you are about to do something for the first time? Do you ever feel too shy to approach someone with a problem and help her? Are you quick to make assumptions about other people's actions and slow to forgive hurts?

By looking within and quietly thinking over her feelings, Estee was able to find comfort when she was about to do something for the first time. There are times when everyone will have to do something they have never done before. This occurs when we go to a new camp, begin studying in a new school, or apply for a job. How did Estee find harmony within?

"*True harmony is inner harmony.*" *After searching for ways to attain inner peace the answer came to me. I asked myself, "Why is a child so content? Why doesn't he worry? Why is it that the adults are the ones with all the anxiety?" A child who has a problem feels soothed by the fact that his father will help him. A frightened child will feel secure if he holds his father's hand. He knows that his father is there to rescue him. If he faces a problem he knows that in the long run, everything will be good. After all, his father only wants the best for him.*

As a child matures, he realizes that his father is human. As much as he loves him, he cannot control everything that happens to him. At this point one's peace of mind might become disturbed. One may feel frightened or depressed when he or she wonders,

"Who will save me now?"

We would never feel frightened or distressed, however, if we would realize that Hashem is our real Father, a Father with ultimate power. He can protect us forever. Hashem is a Father who only wants what is good for us. Having faith gives us true peace of mind. It can make you feel like a different person. Here is an example of a time when it helped me.

This past Succos, I went to Eretz Yisroel for the first time. I had never traveled overseas and I had a fear of flying. As I stepped onto the plane, the fear began to grow stronger and stronger. I told myself, "Hashem wants what is best for me. I am His child and whatever He does will be good for me, even if it might seem bad at the time, so why be scared?" It is unbelievable how well it worked! My fear subsided and I felt calm. Now whenever I am scared, I say these words to myself. The effects are immediate.

It also leads to gratitude. Once you realize that your Father loves you and does everything for your good, you begin to love Him and appreciate all He gives you. I recommend it for all types of anxiety. It's the best remedy!

Estee B.

Sharing the Pain

Comforting someone who is in pain is a distressing responsibility. I know the feeling. When I realize I'll have to make a *shivah* call — visit someone who has lost a family member — I try not to go alone. I usually remember the visit for a few days and sometimes I can't sleep at night.

From inside the small, dimly lit room where our friend is sitting on a low stool, we look at the world differently. At this moment nothing else in the world is as important as bringing relief to our friend in whatever small way we can. We want so much to make the pain stop but we can't. Yet when we reach out and show our interest and concern we are helping. As distressing as her pain is, she will feel better because she didn't have to face it alone. Feeling the love of family and friends will help this person weather the storm and give her the courage to face the future.

Often the things that are most difficult for us bring out a strength we didn't know we had. We tend to panic when we first face a complex situation and wonder how we will cope. However, when we look back we realize that we've become refined through the experience. We go beyond our mundane concerns when we deal with deeper things in life. Showing our interest in others gives us a sense of purpose.

Even if we wonder what we will say or whether or not it will help, it's important to try. There were several occasions when I cooked and brought food to someone who was mourning for a family member who had passed away. The first time I did it I felt an unexplainable timidity. However, going back a few times and being able to offer tangible help gave me a sense of purpose. I'll always remember helping in this way when it was really needed. Our friendship has not been the same since I brought those meals over. Before we were casual acquaintances; now we are friends.

Sara never imagined her self-sufficient friend would need her. She always thought that being supportive in a difficult situation is something that someone else does. Supporting someone who is going through an ordeal is tough. She felt inadequate but she had to jump in and just be there.

*W*hen I was younger I never imagined that there were any benefits to a difficult situation except for hard work. When I grew older I realized that good things can result from them.

The parent of a girl who is in my grade but in a different school got very sick in the beginning of the year. We were constantly davening and hoping that Hashem would make him well.

One dreary day in November on our way out to buy lunch, the sad news came that unfortunately this parent was not among us anymore. My friend is very close with this girl. She broke down and began sobbing and screaming, "NO! NO! NO!" She was wrought-up and leaning on me and crying.

My initial thought was, "I can't handle this situation. I don't know what to say. What should I do?" My friend was hysterical and her whole body was shaking. I looked around and realized that there was no one else and that she really needed me. I found myself gaining strength. I began soothing my friend and helping her to calm down. "Let's go to the office," I suggested. I explained the situation and asked for permission for her to go home and attend the funeral.

Afterwards I was amazed that I had managed to do something that I had never dreamed I was capable of doing. I realized the benefit of a difficult situation is that you find strength within you that you hadn't envisioned before.

Sara B.

The message is evident. The love and support of family and friends is a foundation of the universe. We can't survive alone. Every person will reach out for support at some point in her life. Instead of being discouraged by the pain others are facing, ask yourself, "How can I help? What small thing can I do to help those who are hurting? In what ways can I reach out?" Now, with every word and deed you can make an important difference.

Attitude Matters

How do you view your problems? Do you look at problems as though they were placed before you to make you miserable? Do you give up and drop the problem in the lap of another person who you think is more capable? Do you feel discouraged and decide that it doesn't even pay to try?

If you are a person with a negative attitude, every problem becomes magnified. A problem becomes an excuse to give up.

On the other hand, if you are a person with a positive attitude, you feel challenged by a problem. Perhaps there is a reason that this had to happen. Perhaps something good will come out of this troublesome predicament. The problems in your life test your courage, intelligence and determination. With persistence you can grow by dealing with a difficult situation.

Is the cup half full or half empty?

One summer we were redoing our basement. The basement hadn't been touched since the day we moved in six years ago.

The contractor started by pulling out the panels from the walls. As he was finishing, he suddenly gave a yelp. We came running. We saw two things in there—a wallet and a dead mouse! We quickly got rid of the mouse by dumping it in the rubbish. Then we opened the wallet. Wow! There was close to $1,000 inside. We felt like we had won the lottery.

Later, when my brothers came home, my mother told them that the contractor found something in the basement. My mother asked, "Can you guess what we found?"

One brother said, "Oh, you probably found a mouse." The other brother guessed, "Maybe you found a pot of gold."

There are optimists and pessimists. At different times one or the other will be right. It is still more pleasant to live with an optimist.

R.S.

*E*ven when something bad happens there can be a benefit in it as well. Mrs. X was undergoing surgery. In middle of the operation, while she was sedated, she saw an image of the Lubavitcher Rebbe. The Rebbe told her that if the doctor will put on tefillin, his daughter will recover.

As soon as Mrs. X. awakened from surgery she called the doctor and told him what she had seen. The doctor said, "My daughter is very sick and they can't find a cure for her. I've been searching for a sign that my daughter will live. What you saw was a sign that my daughter will get better."

This doctor's daughter did recover and he puts on tefillin every day.

Fraidy F.

༄

*O*ne night Chany was lying in bed on the lower bunk and her brother was on the top of their bunk bed. They were both very tired, so each of them suggested that the other one get up to turn off the light. After five minutes of arguing, Chany decided to turn off the light. As she got out of bed there was a loud "bang, crash, boom!" The top bed had fallen down on the very spot she had been lying on only moments earlier! Chany is alive today to tell the story. God watches us at every moment.

Rochel Leah R.

༄

*E*veryone faces problems every day. However, when you hear that someone did an exceptional deed, it helps you cope. It makes you feel positive about life. A mother was helping the yeshiva at its Chinese Auction. Many people came and went, contribulting their donations of different sums. Since everyone was *on line it was pretty crowded. One lady called the mother to come to the side. She said, "I'd like to donate $2,000 to the yeshiva but please do not tell anyone that it was me who gave this donation." As the lady walked away the mother thought, "This lady is a rose who definitely made my day."*

Chanie S.

Reaching Out to Others

The Torah way of thinking is that each individual is not an isolated island. We are all connected to other Jews in one grand unit. We should look for ways to share our hearts, our time, our talents and our resources.

Once we recognize that everything we have is a gift from Hashem, we realize that we have to search for ways to help others. We can approach others by saying kind words, by smiling or by doing a favor. Our Sages tell us that doing acts of kindness is one of the pillars that upholds the world. We should want to give. Giving gives us pleasure and a feeling of accomplishment.

The kindness in your heart is revealed in many ways. Sometimes you help a stranger. You may smile and say a compliment to someone you met a minute ago. Perhaps you regularly visit someone in a nursing home, even on a rainy day, although you only know her first name. This morning you may have picked up the forgotten notebooks of the girl sitting next to you on the bus.

We often help people we know well. Although there are ten girls in the bunk, you may be the one who will order the birthday cake topped with lots of love for your friend. When everyone rushes home after a party, you may be the one who stays to help the hostess clean up. If there is someone who doesn't have a partner for a dance, you may be the one who notices and, with a smile, offers a friendly hand. Being there for our sisters, our nieces and nephews and our grandparents is also a great kindness.

While interviewing several teens about the various acts of kindness they did, I discovered a magic ingredient that giving to others has given them. These girls related that satisfaction and happiness is a natural result of giving to others. One realizes how wealthy and fortunate they actually are after helping someone else.

When you give from the heart; when you do not give for recognition but because you sincerely care; when you give quietly without waiting, looking, asking or expecting anything in return, a gift comes back to you. Yitty described that when they left the hospital or nursing home they were singing inside. Yitty realized that she began paying closer attention to everyday joys after visiting Blanche.

QUESTION: *Can you think of a time when you really felt good about visiting the chronic care facility?*

YITTY: Every Friday morning for two years I went to the chronic care facility to help Blanche. We had a talk the week before her death. Blanche told me that at the age of twenty she had a bad cough. The cough lasted a long time and when she finally went to check it out she was informed that she was becoming paralyzed. She did the best she could, given her situation.

QUESTION: *Why did Blanche need your help?*

YITTY: Blanche was paralyzed from her neck down. Essentially she couldn't move past her bed. Yet she was a remarkable person.

QUESTION: *In what way did you gain by visiting Blanche?*

YITTY: Every week I came face to face with Blanche's determination and courage. I looked forward to these visits. She was someone you wanted to be near. This year Blanche passed away. A week before her death I was by her bed. She asked me to put a few things away. She had an exact place for everything and she asked me to organize all her belongings. She always said, "Yitty, you can learn from me to be neat." And I did.

QUESTION: *How can you tell that Blanche appreciated what you were doing for her?*

YITTY: Before I left she always thanked me. She said, "I want to see you again. You helped me a lot. "

QUESTION: *Why was visiting Blanche worthwhile?*

YITTY: Blanche left a deep impression on me. She had been in her bed for about forty years, yet she always had a smile on her face. She was not able to move, yet she kept her life going. She prayed every day, greeted every visitor cheerfully, and kept an immaculate room. When I think of Blanche I feel determined to be grateful for many things. Even the simple gift that I can move my hands and feet.

Yitty W.

⁓

The way in which we see the world shapes our responses to the trials life presents. A sense of gratitude helps us to choose wisely ... what we say, what we do, how we feel. How preposterous for us—who are richer and consume 10 times the resources than 95 percent of the world's people, who routinely live 25 years longer than our great-grandparents, who enjoy freedom of religion — to focus on the empty half of the glass.

I have a neighbor who is blind. I often go to visit her. One afternoon I knocked on the door. I heard a few loud crashes. After a while, she finally came to the door. I asked her if she was all right. She assured me that nothing out of the ordinary had happened and she was fine. I realized that just walking through the house presented obstacles for her. How fortunate are we who have our sight.

Malky O.

⁓

One of our frequent visitors is a young married woman who had polio. She can only walk with crutches. Her husband also walks with crutches. Once while I was escorting them home on Shabbos it began to rain. I unconsciously began to quicken my pace. I noticed that my guests were trying to jump quicker on their crutches but couldn't. As I slowed down, I realized that I really have to be grateful for my health.

Faigy F.

I came into class one day and found a "Kindness newsletter" on every desk. I started reading. There was a paragraph about an elderly woman who was looking for someone to take her to shul every Shabbos. It said that the girl who used to take her is now studying in Israel. I looked at the address and discovered that she lived around the corner from my house. The phone number was listed as well. I couldn't wait to get home and call her.

I called as soon as I got home. The phone was busy for a while. Finally I got through. We decided that I would pick her up at 10:15, walk to the synagogue, and then I would take her back home about two hours later.

Since I started doing this every week I feel that I've changed. Our walks are so meaningful and very encouraging. She is over ninety years old and she tells me amazing stories as we walk. On Purim I sent her Mishloach Manos and it made her so happy. She was very excited to give me one in return.

She struggles to go to the synagogue even though she can't see. Her determination is an inspiration.

Rachely K.

In Her Own Words

I remember an experiment my teacher in eighth grade once did with us that had a very big effect on me. She told us about a girl who lost one of her arms but lives normally and does everything everyone else does.

My teacher told us not to use one of our arms for an entire day and see what would happen. It was difficult and frightening at the same time. I tried putting my hair into a ponytail, but I couldn't manage it by myself with one hand. I needed help. I tried making a salad with one hand when I got home. Once again I needed help. Even simply clearing the table took twice as long as it normally would.

This experiment taught me a tremendous lesson. I learned to appreciate what I have so much more. We take so much for granted. The fact that we wake up and all of our body parts are intact is a tremendous blessing. We should take the things we think are "little" and realize that they are a tremendous kindness from Hashem.

Malka Flaumenbaum

When I first begin talking about complaining less and enjoying each day of life more, people don't always understand my message. Often people wonder what I am excited about. Grumbling is pretty widespread. I know someone who always looks at the good in life. She believes that whatever Hashem has given her is truly a gift. She maintains that she enjoys many benefits. This person has traveled, spoken to large audiences and met many important people. Everyone is amazed to find out that this person is blind. If she is content, what are *we* complaining about?

QUESTION: *Does your blindness cause you to feel secluded?*

ANSWER: Thank God everyone is so nice to me. If there is something happening, they try very hard to explain it to me. Sometimes I feel a little bad because everyone is always doing favors for me, but otherwise I'm basically the same as everyone.

QUESTION: *Are you afraid to sit outside alone because you don't know who is coming?*

ANSWER: First, as I told you, everyone is so nice to me. Therefore, there's usually never a need to go out by myself. When I do have to go out alone, thank God, God has given me an extra sense. When someone passes I can practically feel if they mean good or bad.

QUESTION: *How do you always smile and look so cheerful?*

ANSWER: I really don't understand your question. Why shouldn't I smile? If a person would have as much good done for them as I have, they would also always smile. I have so much to thank God for. God could have made me blind from birth. Instead God gave me a gift and allowed me to have vision until I was in eighth grade. When I was 14, I was hit by a car and lost my vision as a result of my injuries. At least I was able to learn many important things before that, such as colors.

My friend accomplishes so much. There are many people who have full vision and they don't do as much as she does. How is she so cheerful? Do you think that she doesn't have problems? When I think about it, it's unbelievable. Although there are many things she will never be able to do, she focuses only on the good in her life. My friend has taught me to view life from an entirely different perspective.

Decisions

What do you do when you have a problem? If you share it with others, you're probably going to hear a lot of helpful hints. Your mother, sister and friend may each have a different opinion.

Sometimes the people you ask can be quite determined that their point of view is definitely right. When people tell you what you should do about your predicament, say, "Thank you for your recommendations. They'll help me make up my mind."

There are many times that I was advised to give up. I applied for a job many years ago and the interview was difficult. The employer said no. Afterwards, I began writing my first book. I showed my first chapter to a freelance editor. His opinion was negative and discouraging. I got to work and produced a first book, then a second, a third, a fourth and now the fifth, Baruch Hashem. When people give you advice it's important to remember that you still have a choice whether or not to listen.

When my earliest manuscript was complete I asked my aunt, who is a professor of journalism, to read it. I fondly remember her encouraging words. I'm glad I listened to her advice. "Don't wait for your book to be perfect, publish it now. There are writers who keep a book in a drawer for years. Publish it! Your next books will be even better."

I savored each heartening word. My aunt said the next ones would be better. Could it be that I'd manage to write more than one book? I felt that those gentle guiding words were lifting me up.

I've discovered there are two kinds of people who give advice. There are those who show off by explaining that you are just a beginner and those who look for ways to show you that you can do something important.

Consider all the advice people give you. If one suggestion seems great, use it! If some suggestions are good, combine them and use them. If there are suggestions that aren't good don't use them. Don't let people make you feel bad for not following their advice. Suggestions are just ideas to help you make up your mind. You make the final resolution.

If there is something you would love to do that seems impossible right now, dream and pray to Hashem for help. Be willing to understand your smallness and greatness simultaneously. We are all partners with the Creator. Things happen through you, yet your life is entirely in the Creator's hands. Nothing is known beforehand. Even as you strain to climb higher, look at your accomplishments so far and value them. They are precious. They are a miracle.

Expect to be surprised. As Reb Mendel Kaplan said, "Be careful what you pray for, you just might get it."

Part 2

Inspiration

Thinking About Inspiration

Is there any feeling more thrilling than inspiration? How does inspiration send up its slender shoots through the dense and rocky soil of despair and around the weeds of regret?

- When have feelings of inspiration caught you unaware?
- When has a song given you a special feeling of comfort and connection with Hashem?
- Have you ever suddenly realized that although nothing seems to have changed outwardly, everything is different?
- What is the greatest miracle that has happened to someone you know?
- What wonderful example of Hashem's guidance have you experienced this month?
- Does inspiration occur only once in a rare while or can it be accessed every day, at any moment?
- Do you feel that inspiration is hard to achieve? Do you feel distant yet yearn to connect with God?

Actually, inspiration is simpler and closer to you than you think it is.

My son came home from school and said that his English teacher had announced, "Do you want a special blessing that will help you attain success in life? It will also help you succeed in the test next period. If so, come to me before class." My son had walked over. He was curious. The teacher said, "Simply go to the water fountain and before you take a drink of water, say the customary blessing—*Shehakol Nehiya B'dvoro*—which means that everything exists because of God's will. However, this time when you say the blessing, pause for a minute and consider what each word mean."

The Kosel

Few of us will enjoy the thrill of visiting this place today, but all of us can open a siddur. When we stand to pray we face a certain direction. We direct our prayers to a specific spot. Every Jew in the world faces the same site. We all channel our prayers to a place in the world that is closer to heaven than it is to earth.

Have you ever visited this ancient wall? Have you ever prayed as you stood and gazed at the huge gray and beige stones? When you are there you feel different. You reach upward on tiptoe and a part of you that you weren't aware of comes forward. You are at the source. All blessings descend to the world through this place. Holiness is filtered through these ancient stones to the world. Your inner being stands on tiptoe. You become aware of the particle of greatness in you.

As you reluctantly step back from the wall with slow steps, a question lingers in your mind – How can I take this experience and keep its presence with me permanently?

ം

The first time I stood in front of it, it loomed over me like a great tower with no end. I retreated in awe with my heart hammering inside me, but I was drawn forward again. I fell toward the Kosel's ancient stones. I hugged the stones and caressed them. I traced over the cracks worn from the tears of years ago and I was filled with emotion. I was finally standing in front of the Kosel!

On Shabbos, I observed throngs of Jews from all over the world. People flowed endlessly toward this holy place. There was a magnetic force pulling them toward the Kosel. I had never seen so many different Jews united in one place. It was spellbinding. I observed how this one place brought Jews together from the four corners of the earth.

Every day before I pray I imagine that I'm in front of the

Kosel. This thought helps me concentrate and I have a desire for the Geulah. Since that visit, I have never forgotten the throngs of people at the Kosel. We are all striving for one goal. May the Redemption come in our days.

Esther Mindy L.

⸘

Open your siddur and let the words take you on a wonderful expedition. You will journey through history as you sing the same words of praise that our forefathers sang when the Red Sea split. You will voyage to many places as you sing the words that King David composed. Perhaps you will boldly go where you've never gone before, investigating your own connection to Hashem, the impact of your emotions on your actions and the importance of nurturing your inner life. Of course you wish you could take a trip to the Kosel Hamaarovi right now, but even in your own home you can still leave the ordinary world behind each time you pray. Simply think about the words you are saying in a personal manner. After praying you will have a changed perspective.

Be an Inspiration

You may already be an inspiration and not even know it. We seldom influence others with words. We inspire by sharing a piece of our heart. People are moved by our actions. Afterward, when they have the opportunity they may aim for something more as well.

When you begin even in a small way, you can produce a powerful effect. You don't need to control others—just be an example.

Others see you and they realize that many wonderful things are possible. Sometimes you will hear that someone has done a great thing because she learned from you—often you won't remember. Have you ever wished you could change the world? It may be in a major or minor way. It may affect many people or just a few. All this can be done with one decision. You could change the world by deciding to organize a helpful organization. Someone's life may change because of your decision.

Someone I know decided to collect all her tapes and put them in order. After a few weeks of enjoying her tapes she had an idea: Why not lend her tapes out to others? That way others can appreciate the music as well.

After her decision she spent many hours preparing labels for each tape. She posted signs around the neighborhood to advertise her service. It began slowly. At first only a few people came to borrow tapes. Eventually, her library gained popularity. She had to buy more tapes to keep the large crowd supplied. It was extremely satisfying to help others with barely any effort. Her decision to lend tapes helped many others.

An inspired decision can lead to something very productive.

Esti F.

Everything that happens to us can be a lesson from the Almighty. When we open our eyes we can learn from everyday occurrences. Our lives become more peaceful when we realize that even our smallest mitzvos are significant. There is a blessing in everything that happens to us, and an opportunity for growth. As we proceed through life we should say, "Thank you," in our mind, "Thank you," in our heart and "Thank you," with our mouth.

Our world changes as we begin to share the love that the Almighty continually bestows upon us. Hashem asks of us that we love one another and be kind to one another. Remember that every face reflects the presence of God. In this way, ordinary conversations with people we meet can bring us closer to God.

༺༻

Although he was ill and very weak, Rabbi Yechezkel Sarna, Rosh Yeshiva of Chevron, exerted himself one Saturday night a few weeks before his death, to go to the yeshiva to pray Maariv. As he was walking up the steps, he and the person accompanying him realized that the students had finished praying. Nevertheless, Rabbi Sarna continued up the steps.

"Why are you troubling yourself?" asked his companion. "They have already finished praying."

"Praying with the congregation is the fulfillment of a rabbinical obligation, but blessing a student to have a good week is the fulfillment of 'Love your fellow man' which is a Torah commandment," said Rabbi Sarna.

(*Marbitzai Torah Umussar* and *Love Your Neighbor*)

༺༻

•❖ Just One Word

She must have been around five years old. She was sitting on the steps with a desperate look on her face. Her narrow eyes, small nose and round face were the only signs of her disability. She had Down's Syndrome.

She caught my glance as I was passing and I said a cheerful, "Hello!" Her eyes suddenly brightened and a huge smile spread across her face as she yelled back a loud, "Hello!"

Every day I passed her house on my way home. There she would be, sitting on the steps. Would she remember me, I wondered? As soon as she saw me she came stumbling down the steps and gave me a big hug. It was a little embarrassing, but I felt I had accomplished something important. That one little word meant a lot to her.

Every day the little girl sat on the steps waiting for me to come by and say "Hello." Every day she smiled and shouted back.

It was just one word.

Confidential Kind Act

I was boarding the city bus home from school. A young boy boarded the bus before me. He didn't have money to pay, and the driver yelled at him to pay more next time, but let him on anyway. I gave the driver enough money for two people and told him that it was for the boy. That boy never knew that I did this for him. I felt proud to do something nice for someone without getting any recognition from anyone. I learned from that experience that it's easy to do something nice, and it's more fulfilling when you do it to be kind and not so people will think you are nice.

Sara L.

Determination is Important

The ordinary activities that we do daily often hide important lessons. Determination gives us a sense of purpose. Holding on to our goals and aspirations despite difficulties helps us feel that we are growing. I can visualize determination concretely because I saw it every Thursday night.

Every Thursday night, my mother made compote. She hunted in the refrigerator for bruised or old pears and apples. I sat near her at the table and watched her peel the fruit. She did not use a vegetable peeler but she peeled the apples perfectly with an ordinary knife. The peel was paper thin and it was a perfect, long spiral. One spiral after another would magically emerge from my mother's knife. I watched her and wondered how she did it.

Afterwards, my mother would check the apples and pears and cut away the brown parts. She usually assured me that no one would know that the original apple was less than perfect. I felt that I had an important secret to keep. I promised not to divulge the information about how the apple looked before it entered my mother's pot.

After the fruits were in the pot my mother added water so that they shouldn't turn brown. Then she opened a box of prunes and cut each one and took out the pits. She also checked each prune. I don't remember that my mother ever found anything; but I knew you always check. Before she added the sugar my mother said, "L'kavod Shabbos Kodesh."

My mother worked from Sunday to Thursday from 8:00-5:30. I remember the delicious homemade food we ate each Shabbos. I've begun wondering, *Why? Why did my mother invest so much effort to prepare the Shabbos food herself? Why did she wake up at 6:00 A.M. on Thursday to make Shabbos fish? Why did she make this compote at a late hour on Thursday night?*

I've concluded that it comes down to two things. First, determination is everything. My mother felt that Shabbos has to be honored with food cooked fresh, from scratch, and she was determined not to take shortcuts. My mother could have gone around the corner and purchased our Shabbos food at Meal Mart, but she cooked for Shabbos because she wanted to cook.

The second and perhaps more important reason that my mother made compote every Thursday night is because she was determined not to waste food. This wasn't because it is important to be thrifty. It wasn't because buying fresh fruit was too expensive. Taking care not to waste food is something worth doing because it's a mitzvah.

The other day I cleaned the fridge and found some smashed pears and apples that had bumps. It was an hour before Shabbos and it was too late to make compote. With a sigh I threw them out. I knew no one would eat them anymore. I remembered that my mother made compote every week so that she would be able to use up all the old fruit and not throw food away. I think that next week I'll begin making compote.

Inspiring Others

When you are excited about an ideal you become a radiating source of light to others.

People are afraid to preach to others. No one wants to stand out and be different even if it's for something good. However the words you offer are not important. It's important to simply act upon your ideals. The more of yourself you offer to something the more consideration you will receive in return.

Other people follow. They don't necessarily follow what you say. They follow what you are and what you do. You don't need to control others to motivate them. You can become the source of substantial good when you set an example — when you do the right thing.

- *What sort of role model do I want to be?*
- *How do I want others to see me?*
- *What beliefs and values do I stand for?*
- *How do I want to be remembered?*
- *In twenty years when my classmate says, I remember her from eleventh grade ... How would I want her to complete that sentence?*

෴

The Bobover Rebbe, Rav Shlomo Halberstam, had suddenly fallen ill. I walked into the classroom with a box that contained all of the 150 chapters of *Tehillim* divided into 24 booklets. As the girls did their in-class assignment, I prayed. I said, "If you finish early and you would like to take a booklet, we will be able to finish the *Tehillim* together."

My students used the opportunity well. Everyone took a booklet. The room was filled with whispers in the silence. We became a united group. I had shared a spark of emotion and it generated a flame of inspiration. Everyone felt that something precious had occurred in the room.

Over the weeks the Bobover Rebbe slowly gained strength and I continued to bring the box. Then a girl came up to my desk with a small smile and glowing eyes that revealed her innermost character. "Mrs. Weinreich, how can I acquire a box of booklets like yours? The girls on my block meet on Shabbos and I'd like to complete the *Tehillim* with my friends each week."

I realized then that something simple had turned into a miracle. I looked upon my student with admiration and pride. I had never exhorted, commanded or dictated a rule. The spontaneous interest surprised me. It continued to grow. After that first request many girls came forward and asked to begin their own groups. There were at least thirty new groups that began in those two months.

Something permanent has remained between us. The energy that was generated by those earliest heartfelt prayers was multiplied and magnified. The twelfth graders see me and come to greet me. "Mrs. Weinreich, our group has continued. We still come together each week to finish the *Tehillim*." "Mrs. Weinreich, a friend was visiting from Lakewood; she'd like to start a group too."

Know that when you begin something idealistic, a powerful connection is established. You don't have to control others. You need only be an example. Your positive action can inspire and produce an effect on many.

Reflections on Birthdays

Every birthday is a milestone. Before you started school each birthday made you feel much bigger and more grown-up. Do you remember when someone asked you to show them on the fingers of your hand how old you were?

A birthday is a time to feel grateful. You may think back to stories you heard about your first months of life. Thank Hashem that you are here. Thank your parents too. Perhaps this should be their day of celebration also.

There is a feeling of wonder within you on your birthday. You smile before you realize why you are happy. You may decide with determination that a new year and a new start awaits you. You aren't going to simply continue on the same path as last year. You feel energy within to run toward new goals and climb higher than ever before.

•❖ *Bas Mitzvah Day*

I woke up early on my birthday. This was not a birthday like all others. This was my twelfth birthday. I would now become a Bas Mitzvah. I would become responsible for all of my actions. Although I was quite nervous about the great responsibility which would now be placed upon my shoulders, I couldn't wait for the attention I'd be receiving. I imagined all eyes centered on me. I would be the star. I lay in bed dreaming of my special day. I heard the slow breathing of my younger sister as she slept in the bed nearby.

As the morning sun peeked through my shades I jumped out of bed. I usually don't get up this early, but on my twelfth birthday I wanted to have an early start. I wanted to have extra time to pray with more precision. As my prayers ended I found myself fervently whispering Shehecheyanu in my heart. I thanked Hashem for bringing me to this particular moment.

Esther Z.

✒ A Different Celebration

*T*wo weeks before my birthday my mother said, "You can celebrate in whichever way you want. You can choose a formal, fancy party, or an intimate family meal. You name it! It's up to you."

Did I want a small party at home with my friends? Did I want a night out in a fancy restaurant with my parents? A big party, in a catered hall with all my cousins, also sounded nice. My mother had told me I had two days to decide and I spent two sleepless nights reviewing my options.

After 48 hours I told my parents my decision. They were surprised. They asked, "Are you sure?" I said, "Yes, I've positive." I decided on one thing—nothing. I told my parents to take the money they would have spent on my party and donate it to tzedakah for someone less fortunate than me.

Goldy H.

Growing and Changing

A birthday is a special day. It's a landmark occasion you want to honor. Sometimes you celebrate with family. Perhaps your friends remember your birthday and celebrate with you too.

A birthday is also a time to think about many different things. Has this year made a difference? What terrific things have happened for you? What wonderful plans do you have to look forward to? These are questions that are always there, but they come to the forefront on your birthday.

Sometimes a birthday is a time to decide to change. We may not change our activities very much but we can change the way we look at things. We may decide to incorporate something extra into our daily routine. A birthday is a particularly good time to contemplate how much you've grown and how far you have come. Remember, however, that reflecting and taking stock is something we can do at **any** time.

When you contemplate the possibility of changing and growing, you can have conflicting feelings. It may comfort you to realize that it is normal to have this inner battle. We all share the same problem. Changing our character or outlook can be a creative task, but it can also be difficult. Rav Yisroel Salanter explains that improving one's character is a mammoth task, more difficult than mastering the entire Talmud. The Yetzer Hara continually attempts to sabotage potential holiness.

Sometimes it's good to stop and reflect. It can be encouraging to take stock of the ways you've already changed and matured. You should ask yourself, "What do I do right?" Before you can investigate new goals, maintain a harmonious balance by contemplating that which you already have accomplished. Before groaning about the fact that you haven't yet learned to play an instrument, congratulate yourself for developing your dancing talent. Don't say, "I'm not good at that"; instead think of the many things you are good at. A person goes from strength to strength.

*W*hen I was young I loved to visit an elderly lady in an old-age home. My mother would go every week and I always begged to come along. I enjoyed speaking to all the old people and watching them light up with happiness every time we came. We always brought some homemade cake or kugel, which they truly appreciated. Somehow I always felt that I got more out of these meetings than the old people. I felt grateful for everything I have and can do.

Sury F.

*W*hen I was younger I adored the mirror. I would sit in front of the mirror and play beauty parlor with my sisters. I would make funny faces and talk to my image. I thought there was another person in the mirror. On the street whenever we passed a glossy new car I would steal a quick glance. As I got older I realized that looking at others is more interesting than looking at myself.

Malky O.

*A*s a child I loved elevators. I thought that they were safe and that escalators would eat me up. Now the whole situation has changed. I hate elevators because if they get stuck you can't get out. If an escalator gets stuck you can just skip up the steps. So you see, life changes. What you may like today, you make dislike tomorrow.

Elka Rochel M.

As a child I loved to sit on my grandfather's lap. Every Sunday he came to my house. We played games together. I'd sit on his lap and he'd read me a story and give me nosh. I still enjoy my grandfather's visits, but in a different and more mature way.

Malkie S.

∽∾

When I was a child I loved to laugh. I used to laugh so much that I laughed all day long. One day while I was eating, I guess I laughed too much. I began choking on my food. Since then I only laugh when it is necessary.

Avigail Z.

∽∾

As a child I loved following my older sister. Wherever she went I went. Whatever she did I did. When she went to her friend's house, her shadow followed her. I finally realized that it was a silly thing to do. I should have a life and a mind of my own. We are two different people. Why should I get yelled at since I'm following my sister? I should find ways to have my own fun.

Nechama Liba M.

∽∾

When I was a child I loved to dance. Whenever I was allowed to, I'd put on lively music and dance to it. Most of my friends had other pastimes at that age, but I stuck to dance.

When dance tryouts for our high school play were announced I wondered, "Should I try out or not?" I followed my impulse and tried out. I was accepted!

Today I'm happy I always danced when I was younger because this helped me develop my dancing talent.

Chanie B.

⸙

As a child I had a lively imagination. My reflection was my friend. The little girl in the mirror was my companion. I'd talk and smile and a "real person" smiled back. When I got older I realized it was me in the mirror. I also realized that I have to be my own best friend.

Chani K.

⸙

When I was a child I adored stationery. Trading stationery was my favorite hobby. I would go to a friend's house and deal with my stationery as if I were engaged in a vital business deal. I had a large, colorful, flowery album in which I kept my treasures. The album was full of old and new stationery. "Hello, Kitty" and Israeli stationery were my favorites.

As I grew older, I passed my treasure to my younger sister, who now derives full pleasure from the "treasure" of my youth.

⸙

When I was younger I loved to listen to tapes before I went to sleep. My parents placed a tape recorder near my bed and I'd lie under the covers and listen to my favorite story tapes. In my mind I would visualize all the events I was hearing about. I believe that this love for stories has helped me become a very good storyteller today.

Surie W.

A Box

I entered the classroom with one big carton from U.P.S. and one small white box imprinted with the bakery's logo. My students knew that something interesting was about to occur.

"Good afternoon, girls." I said. "I'd like to tell you about my great-aunt, Rivka Perlman, *O"H*. It was the last year of her life. She was frail, often exhausted and suffered severe pain because of a terminal illness. Yet she succeeded in hiding her infirmity. At nine in the morning on Succos I came to escort her to shul but it took her longer than usual to get ready. We left at about ten minutes before eleven o'clock. As we crept along slowly my aunt repeated the refrain, 'I hope we arrive on time. It's late and I wish I had strength to hurry.'

"Finally we stood in front of the steps to the synagogue. We walked up and I pulled the brown, heavy metal door open. From the back of the women's section my aunt heard the *chazan* say the last words of the *Shemone Esrei*. She turned to me with a radiant, eager face. I had never seen this degree of spontaneous rejoicing before. 'Roiza, we made it. We are in time for Hallel!' I handed her the prayer book. I bent down to draw my prayer book out of the bag and find the correct place. When I looked up my aunt was gone!

"In a moment she had sped to her place in the front. How? We had crept along slowly, but now she had a sudden spurt of energy.

"There are times in life when I think of Aunt Rivka. On the morning that my baby was born I was in the synagogue, despite the fact that I was in labor. My aunt was in constant pain, yet she had one desire constantly pulsing in her heart. She wanted to say *Hallel*—to thank and praise Hashem.

"Girls, in the past few weeks I've brought a little box of *Tehillim* booklets to school. When you completed your class work you've each taken one booklet. In that way we have been finishing the entire book of *Tehillim* in about ten minutes. Some of you saw the magic of finishing the book of *Tehillim* as a group. You approached and asked me if you could begin a group of your own on your block. Today I'm giving out seven sets of *Tehillim*. This is a wonderful beginning. Seven new groups will meet weekly to complete the entire book of *Tehillim*.

"When I entered the bakery today I saw the exact sugar cookie that my Aunt Rivka preferred. She served them whenever I visited. I remembered Aunt Rivka's joy at the opportunity to pray. I felt it's appropriate that we should celebrate the inauguration of the new *Tehillim* groups by serving her cookies."

◦◦ *Inspiring the World*

Can it really be? Do each of us really make a difference? We may hear about it once but can we then deduce that the phenomenon is more prevalent than we had expected? Hashem has sent me encouragement with the inspiration and effect of the *Tehillim* groups.

I am wonderstruck by the way the gift of the *Tehillim* boxes has grown. There is continuous progress as new groups are initiated. It has grown beyond the scope of my imagination. Each girl continues to meet with her friends every week. The days, months, years go by and in many different places the ideal grows. The chain continues when someone in the group decides to take a box and start a different group somewhere else.

I watch as new miracles unfold. A generous, spirited personality walks up to my desk after the class completed the *Tehillim* together. She has decided that this is something she can do.

"I didn't realize. Look, there is an 800 number on the back. I'm going to call and ask if I can start my own group."

"I'm going to Montreal for Shavuos. I told my aunt about this project and she said, 'Bring a box of booklets along.'" The boxes are going to new places, places where I've never been.

It only takes ten minutes to complete the Tehillim as a group and alone it would take one person about two and a half hours.

Inspiration is the sound knowledge makes when it sings, the movement knowledge makes when it dances.

Inspiration is a gift from Above. It surprises you when you honor the flame inside you and learn to keep doing good things wherever you are.

Beginning Something New

Somewhere within each of us there is the capability to be creative, imaginative and resourceful. However, somewhere down the line something goes wrong. The spark begins to fade. It's up to us to look within and fan that spark into a flame.

༺༻

I've come to the realization that I'm not the only one who has a hard time beginning a task. I think motivation is generated by action. Once I undertake a task I become absorbed in it. It takes my time and strength, but I feel happy that I'm busy, useful and productive.

At the same time I seek balance. Motivation is extinguished when one tries to do too much at once. I realize that although I may begin with a large goal I can accomplish it by doing it in small steps. For example, I can work on a big project for an hour a day. If I persist that project will be completed. However, beginning it is not always a simple matter.

Before I start I have many thoughts: Perhaps it's not worth all the effort. It will be a lot of difficult work. Will it be appreciated? Who will enjoy it? Why work so hard when you can't be sure of the outcome? However, once I begin, I feel a rush of enthusiasm.

When I began this book I found my motivation had expanded. I felt excited when I wrote an outline and planned a basic structure for the book. The inspiration then became something concrete instead of just an idea. I feel happy just to be writing. I enjoy seeing my ideas take shape on the computer screen.

When I began my first book I decided I'd write just two pages a day, but I would write **every** day. When I completed two pages, it motivated me to do two more pages on the next day. I surprised myself when I realized after a year that I had written a complete book.

Many limitations that *hold us back* are really only cobwebs. Once you begin and stick your hand through you see that there is nothing there. There are many simple changes you can make in your life that don't actually require a lot of time. The important thing is to begin, and then not to quit until you finish.

Holidays

Sometimes we look at our calendar and wait for a specific day to come. We may even count the days that pass and smile as the important day approaches. There are many special days in our lives. How can we make the most of those days? What's the best way to celebrate?

The Jewish calendar has many happy days of celebration. Each Yom Tov has its special foods and customs. You can plan to make these days personally inspiring. A holiday is a time to thank Hashem for the miracles He has done for you and for the entire Jewish nation. Of course on Pesach we thank Hashem for taking us out of Egypt and on Shavuos we thank Hashem for giving us the Torah. We can be grateful for miracles that are happening now as well.

Rosh Hashanah and Yom Kippur

Decide that you will do one mitzvah perfectly. Perhaps you will be careful with the blessings over food. Perhaps you'll buy a sign that has the blessings in large print so that you can read them carefully instead of mumbling the words. (Rav Segal of Manchester always read each blessing over food from a card he carried in his pocket.)

Perhaps you will wash your hands each morning very carefully and with a lot of water. Our Sages say that washing our hands with a lot of water is an assurance for wealth.

Decide that you will pay attention to each word of one paragraph of the prayers. For example, say *Aleinu* for two minutes instead of thirty seconds. Maybe you will be able to do this with more prayers as time goes on.

Succos

When we sit in the succah we can feel that Hashem is always protecting us. Everything is O.K. Everything will be fine. I can be happy with today's good news and hopeful for the future. I can relax and rejoice because Succos is here. Now, in this moment, I can remember that Hashem watches us always.

Pesach

Ask those around you to share the adventures and miracles they have experienced. When you read about a miracle, clip the article and put it in your journal. For example, there have been many bombs that were disabled just in time. People have missed a flight that later crashed. The Gulf War and the Six Day War are well known examples. If you keep your eyes open you'll become aware of many miracles.

Shavuos

Read, *For Love of Torah*. It has many wonderful stories of great sages and ordinary people who demonstrated their love for the Torah. Wake up in the morning and say, "I'm a princess. I'm the daughter of the King of the universe. The world is waiting. I'm giving it a smile. I'm going to pray and do mitzvos in a noble manner."

Trust Your Inner Voice

Now, let us explore a vital lesson in problem-solving. Our intuition is like a light that radiates the wisdom within. Sometimes the honest voice within us guides us. We have to simply be prepared to listen.

The more you listen to your inner wisdom, the more you can live sincerely and help others to do the same. Sometimes this can mean simply stopping what you are doing for a few minutes and reflecting on the larger picture.

In this way the gift of sincerity gets passed on from person to person. If you think you have the ability, try and you will succeed. Trust your heart. When you feel like doing the right thing but you are afraid because of difficulties, don't talk yourself out of it. In the example below a teen shares a true story and a powerful lesson.

Trust in Hashem and a miracle will happen.

•❖ *Smelling Smoke*

People often do not look in their immediate surroundings for the source of a problem. Rather, they tend to believe that the problem is coming from somewhere else. Several days ago something happened that taught me an important lesson: When something is wrong or missing, first check your close surroundings before deciding it's an outside problem.

My friend and I were sitting in my room looking at a photo album. Suddenly there was a smell of something burning. I looked out my window expecting to see one of my neighbors starting up a barbecue. I was surprised that nothing was happening outside. However, as the smell intensified, my friend suggested that I close the window, thus preventing the smell from permeating the house.

*A short while later my younger sister came up. She asked, "What's burning? The house smells like burnt French toast." With a tinge of alarm in her voice she said, "Baily, something in **this** room is burning!" I was about to disregard her comment when she exclaimed, "Oh my, look at your pillow!" As if struck by a bolt of lightning we jumped up. One look at where my pillow was explained it all. It had accidentally been placed on top of the lamp and a big black hole had burnt right through the outer covering to the feathers beneath it. We stood there in the room, our fingers and knees quivering like Jell-O.*

My first thought was—Hashem is kind. The message that echoed off the walls was—first look within.

Baily J.

There are times when we are confronted by a problem and there doesn't seem to be an obvious solution. However here too, when we use our inner wisdom, we might find one thing that we can do differently. That one thing can make a significant difference.

◆ Bus Ride

When I was younger, my mother thought it was important for all of us to do extracurricular activities. Once a week I went to a swimming club with other girls from my neighborhood. We rode on a city bus. Being normal young girls, we made lots of noise and we quarreled, too. There was shoving and screaming on the bus. Suddenly, a short, skinny girl who was about three years older than I stood up and said, "Stop! Let's all sing together." We began singing and soon all the girls were laughing instead of screaming. I was young then but the experi-

ence left a lasting impression on me. You don't have to continue a quarrel just because it began. Instead of expressing yourself in a negative way—there are alternative, positive ways to vent your feelings.

Batsheva S.

Letting the Sunshine Inside

Have you ever met someone who uses a wheelchair? You may feel sympathy or fear for people who lives in this "prison." You may think they do not have the same freedom that you enjoy, and they cannot go wherever they want.

This simply isn't true. It has happened so many times that it must be more than a coincidence. Once I got to know people sitting in the wheelchair I discovered that they don't feel imprisoned at all. With a positive attitude, they grow beyond their limitations and even help others. After all, the body is just a covering. It conceals the remarkable gifts that live inside the person. Handicapped people can't do everything I can do, yet there are many things they can do. What really counts is the inner person.

I treasure my handicapped friends. They have taught me a beautiful perspective of life. More than anyone else they teach me that much more is possible than I had ever imagined. As one handicapped person said, "Tragedy in a life does not have to mean a life of tragedy."

◆ *A Sunny Day*

Shevy sat in the corner of the playground surrounded by her classmates, chatting happily on that warm June day. Her metal wheelchair gleamed in the sunlight, eliciting stares from the younger children. She chose to ignore them, focusing instead on her friends' conversation.

The bell rang. Recess was over. Chatting girls filed into the building, refreshed from their short break. Shevy waited for her teacher to take her up with the elevator. Her eyes sparkled. She looked rejuvenated. As her teacher approached her face broke out into a wide grin. She was happy—happy to go to school, happy to have devoted friends, happy to be alive!

Tova G.

A Gift From Above

When people experience a close call and their lives are saved, there are two alternative ways of viewing the situation. A common reaction is to assume that it was a lucky coincidence. Perhaps this is based on the expectation that the basic gifts of life will always be there. The assumption is that one made the correct decision that help came at just the right moment or that the person who came realized the problem and was able to fix it in time. Although deep down we want to connect with God, this thinking process distances us from Him.

Perhaps there is another view of the same situation that would be more helpful and more appropriate as well. Although we assume that God is "hiding" because we aren't looking for Him, perhaps He is doing many things to help us at this very moment. The correct decision is really an insight granted to us from Above. The help that arrived at just the right moment is the Almighty's messenger. Finally, the person who helped us in time did so because the Almighty was watching over us. In this way a saved life becomes a precious gift from Above. It encourages us and gives us hope. We realize that we are never alone and that our lives are special and important.

Just in Time

On an ordinary cold winter day, the Schwartz family was enjoying their supper. Their grandmother was visiting and she commented that the steam must be broken because it was very cold. As the night progressed the family felt the chill as well and decided to check out the boiler room. Sure enough, they saw that the boiler was not working. They called for emergency *repair service. However, the company couldn't send anyone. The house was getting unbearable so they called persistently. Finally, someone came. The repair man was busy in the basement until late at night. When he finally came up he said, "You should all thank God. If I hadn't come tonight you wouldn't have woken up tomorrow. Your boiler was releasing carbon monoxide!"*

Second Chance

It was an ordinary Monday morning. The teacher called her colleague and said, "I'm leaving now. I'll meet you in the usual place in five minutes."

"I won't be riding with you to work today," Marian said. "My husband is going in that direction so he will be taking me to school."

The teacher unlocked her car door and settled into the front seat. She adjusted the mirror, buckled the seat belt and put her key into the ignition. As she tuned in the classical music station and pulled out of her driveway she glanced at her watch. "It's only 8:10. I should be in school early today," she noted with satisfaction.

As she neared the intersection she saw that the light was green. It felt good not to have to wait for the light. She passed the green light. A small red car suddenly came barreling down the cross street. It crashed right into her passenger side door. Then everything stopped.

The ambulance siren made her open her eyes. Her first words to the paramedics were, "Thank G-d Marian isn't here."

"This is a miracle. You are a fortunate woman. Everything seems fine," a kind man said. "However I think you should go to the hospital for a routine examination. It's better to be sure."

The teacher sat in my Wednesday class a week later and said:

"My car looked like a crumpled ball of aluminum foil. It took Hatzolah fifteen minutes to get me out of the car. It was a miracle. I was able to stand up on my own two feet. I remember screaming. "Thank Hashem Marian decided not to go with me today."

"I know Hashem made a miracle. I was given a second chance. Since then my perspective has changed. I find that there are many more reasons to be happy every day and there's really nothing to complain about. Frequently we are so busy planning and accomplishing that we fail to build ourselves a life. The result of this upheaval is that I feel more serene and content. As the saying goes, 'Life's too short to go through it with a long face.'

Memorable Encounters

Every day we meet people wherever we go. Sometimes we meet people in physical or emotional pain. Can we reach out to those whose pain is greater than our own? Can we find a way to respect them and learn from them?

Consider the amount of hours devoted to ordinary conversation with our neighbors and acquaintances. Everyday encounters can be a source of inspiration. Attaining our objective requires being willing to become personally involved and bravely seeking to learn from the people we meet. Here a participant describes a short encounter that she will remember for a long time.

Numbers

My eyes fell on an old woman's arm. Inscribed there were the blue permanent numbers, a reminder of a dreadful nightmare. Did I realize what her generation had gone through? Each and every person has his or her story. They can all tell how they overcame their troubles. They survived the horrible ordeal of the Holocaust. They didn't succumb to depression, hopelessness or despair. Like a phoenix reborn from the ashes they rebuilt a new life.

We are the products of their spiritual strength. They created a future—us.

R. Gottesman

What actions could you take to demonstrate that you care for others?

Pockets

Our neighbor passes our house at the same time every morning. He is tall and his posture is erect, straight as a rod. He has a long, immaculate, white beard. His long coat is always spotless. He walks like a soldier, looking straight ahead. His demeanor is serious. He's a man who has seen a lot, survived many trials and lived by willpower.

My son notices our neighbor and runs a bit alongside on the sidewalk. Then he stands on the sidewalk, blocking his path. With a serious demeanor, he puts out his hand and says a very polite good morning. The neighbor pauses and looks slowly at the young child from under bushy eyebrows. My son stands there waiting patiently. A brief dialogue begins. My son introduces himself and explains what he is learning in school. The old man and young child have a mature conversation. The old man asks some knowledgeable questions and my son answers carefully. Finally the elderly man reaches into his pocket.

He pulls out a handful of candies. "How many sisters and brothers do you have?"

"Five," my son replies.

The old man counts seven candies into his hand. "Be sure to give them a candy too," he says.

My son starts bouncing up and down. "Thank you! I'll give one to everyone. But Rabbi H., there are seven."

My neighbor smiles, "An extra one for you because you are learning so well."

The soldier continues walking. His erect posture and his willpower impress those who see him. My children, however, know that the large pockets of his long coat are filled with sweetness, love and fun.

Inspiration

Understanding Other People's Needs

When we take a second look, things become clearer to us. We really can trip over our excuses. It's incredible how we can go down paths we never intended to walk. We think we are being careful and weighing our options. We make elaborate judgments so that we will know what to do and be able to take care of others and ourselves. Yet, perhaps we've been confusing the issue.

Sometimes something unexpected occurs. We are suddenly faced with a reality that usually hovers in the back of our minds. We know on some level that God silently plans everything that happens to us, yet now we are faced with that truth. Our beliefs challenge us. How well are we living by them? Do they inspire us?

✽ *A Mother's Passion*

I watched my guest as I began preparing Sunday morning breakfast. It was easy to recognize that she was ready for a special occasion. She wore a black sweater embroidered with black beaded flowers, a nice wig, and three necklaces.

My guest was waiting near the telephone at 8:30, for a moment of closeness to occur. Her son had promised to call at 9:00. She sat by the table with the newspaper in front of her. Although ten minutes had passed she was still on page one.

She looked up when I approached. I began setting the table. "My son is just wonderful," she told me. "Let me see, I have a photo of him right here in my pocketbook." She began rummaging in her large bag. She began taking out various odds and ends. The old pens, tissues, rubber bands and loose change all landed on my table. "Here it is," she said triumphantly.

I admired the picture politely. "He's almost finished his education. He'll have a doctorate in psychology. He'll be graduating in

June." my guest informed me proudly. I could see that she really loved her son.

She looked at her watch again. It was 9:15. "I hope that nothing is wrong." She began to fret.

I began serving breakfast. I placed a roll, salad and coffee in front of my guest. She wasn't touching her food however.

When my watch showed 9:45, I began feeling helpless and impatient. What could I do to put my guest at ease? I tried to start a conversation but my guest answered in tense monosyllables.

Finally, at 10:00 the phone rang. With all the stored up energy of an hour and a half of waiting my guest hurried to answer the phone. The conversation was proper, polite, perhaps a little detached. Was this the usual way the mother and son connected?

"Yes, yes, I'm fine. You didn't realize how late it was? You say that you have plans...It's O.K.... I understand.... Of course you're very busy... Next time we'll definitely meet."

My guest put the phone back and attempted a smile. "I guess I'll see him when I go to New York next month. He has several important appointments today. I understand."

My guest understood her son. I wondered, however, if her son understood her. For his benefit as well as his mother's, I wished they had met today. I wanted him to discern how much his mother cared for him. He was going to be a psychologist but he couldn't comprehend his own mother's love and needs.

Part 3

Family & Friends

Family

Drop a Pebble in the Water ...

Every day we seek to understand what is happening in our lives within the context of our families and our personal relationships. Being a success at home is simple and difficult at the same time. It's simple because it's within everyone's reach every day. It's difficult because our family relationships are intense and close. We can impress those we meet only occasionally, but our families know what we are really like.

Your home is the place where you are not expected to be different. Your family measures you not by your accomplishments but by who you really are. Your terrific test score is less important to your four-year-old sister than the bowl of cereal you got up to serve her when she was hungry. These mundane acts of kindness may not seem significant, but they are the most vital.

You become a different person not in some faraway place but right here, in the most ordinary surroundings. The rare dramatic act is not as important as the small acts of caring that are repeated often. Every instance of kindness makes a difference.

Of all the chapters in the family section, the chapter about grandmothers is the most precious to me. As I write I'm sitting in the dining room and I glance up and see my grandmother's needlepoint picture. Its message of thoughtfulness and caring echoes in the room.

Do we learn as much as we can from our grandmothers or do we put off visiting them? Do we seize the moment or do we let it slip through our fingers? Do we get on the bus and go or do we sigh in our chairs and tell ourselves today we are too busy, perhaps tomorrow? Just decide that this week you will go and you won't put it off.

The first time you decide that you would like to make your family a priority you pick up a pebble. The first time you act—whether you are delighted or disappointed with the results—you throw a pebble in the pond. The pebble sends out tiny, barely visible ripples. Perhaps no one else will notice. However, the girl who threw the pebble in does—if she's paying attention. That is what is important.

Recipe For Harmony

"The words of the wise are heard because they are spoken gently."
(The Talmud)

It's much more difficult to avoid daily disagreements with one's family than with teachers and friends. Different points of view, conflicting needs and impatience can all erupt into quarrels. Before the fight begins, stop and think. Must this issue be discussed? Is this the right time to make demands? How can I phrase my request carefully?

Must this issue be discussed? There are hassles that arise that will be resolved soon. It's not worth it to get excited over trivial daily upsets that don't matter very much in the big scheme of things. Suppose you misplaced an important folder. You feel harried and pressured because you must bring that folder to school and your friend is picking you up in ten minutes. As you search you feel the anger mount inside you. "Who saw my folder?" you almost shout. "I put it right here on the table. Someone always touches my things." You hear your younger sister's voice, "Here it is, on the kitchen counter." A faint memory surfaces. *You* were the one who put it on the counter. You realize you were too quick to react.

I was a new mother and I had gone to visit my cousin and her eight children in their tiny summer bungalow. During the hour that I was there, numerous urgent and distressing moments arose, but my cousin remained calm and in control. Everything seemed to flow with a system. Even when her toddler cried and made a fuss, she spoke to her softly and politely. I thought ruefully about how agitated I was on a daily basis with just my two-year-old and my infant. "What's your secret?" I wondered. "How do you remain calm and in control?" My cousin laughed and replied, "You can't expect to accomplish everything, so you have to decide what's really important."

Is this the right time? We understand that unless it's an emergency we can't run in and wake our parents at 2 A.M. There are other times in the day, however, that are almost as impractical. Before we request something that's difficult to do, we should ask ourselves if it's a convenient time for the other person. If we don't simply want to air our feelings but we want a real solution, it's important to talk when there is time for *both* parties to think clearly. An easy way to find a time that will work for both of you is to say, "I'd like to talk to you for about twenty minutes. When is a good time for you?"

How can I phrase my request carefully? You may not agree with your parents, but you don't have to confront them. Before you speak it's a good idea to know what you are trying to achieve. Your tone of voice, your choice of words, and your feelings can help you achieve a tactful approach.

I've heard many interesting introductions to lectures. One time the speaker was also a professional musician. His introduction was a lesson I will always remember.

☙❧

The violinist stood before the audience. "Let me teach you effective communication," he said. "I will demonstrate with my violin. A girl stomps into her home and slams the door. 'I didn't want these sneakers, I wanted Keds. It's not fair. You never get what I want. I hate these sneakers. They make my feet look fat.'

"Do you want to hear her mother's reply?" The violinist presses hard with his bow against the violin. The audience hears a spine-tingling screech.

"Now let's peek into a different house," the violinist says. "A daughter walks in, 'Mother you work so hard day and night, you do so much for me. You are the best mother a girl could have. I decided to buy you these flowers. Please read the card I wrote for you!' Now let's hear her mother's response." The violinist gently draws the bow across the strings. We hear a pleasant melody.

The audience begins whispering. The violinist chides. "Don't interrupt this mother. She's talking from the depths of her heart."

When parents and children are distressed they often speak in an abrasive manner. Until the problem is recognized and defused, family discussions will continue to escalate into upsetting arguments. Let's remember the wise words of the Talmud, "The words of the wise are heard because they are spoken gently." Let's strive to step back from a quarrel and speak gently.

❧ Walking Together

Whenever I need to get oriented in a new place, I discover which way is west in a special way. This way is connected with a memory from my childhood. I remember walking up to Friday night services at our synagogue with my father. We faced the setting sun as we talked about our experiences of the past week. The sun in our eyes was so bright that sometimes I had to walk in my father's shadow. Walking into the setting sun will always remind me of that special time.

Abigail H.

Savor the Magic

The most basic and precious foundation for sustaining family tranquility is to make time for your younger siblings, nieces, nephews or cousins. We easily get caught up in a vicious cycle; you are too busy to notice your toddler sister or niece but by not relaxing with a tiny child, life threatens to become one boring, stressful day after another.

Relaxation isn't a luxury. It is necessary for your physical and emotional health. One great way to take a break is to enjoy an adorable little one. Take time off to play with a tot. Forget all the pressures as you relax and smile with a youngster who knows how to be completely happy in this precious moment. You will be more efficient when you return to the task at hand.

He was small and wrapped in a little blue blanket. His tiny eyes were shut against the world. I remember the black fuzz on his head, and his tiny shriveled hands were balled up tight. His face was tinged with yellow and red. How sweet! He was a warm precious baby in my married sister's arms. We had waited for months and now we were able to hold him in our arms.

Now that two years have passed, his little hands are no longer balled up. Those hands are now touching and exploring. He's trying to learn everything he can. He gets up on his own two feet and calls, "Mi'am (Miriam) dance! Dance Mi'am!" I stretch out my hands and bend over to grasp his soft little ones and, while holding hands, we spin around the room.

As we spin to the beat I think, "How happy he looks!" His face spreads with a happy grin and the giggles come from deep within. His little nose, big eyes and small mouth are a treasure to cherish.

In the summer he asks me, "Peas (please) can I have ices?" It's hard to say no. I give him his ices and he tells me, "Thank you." I put a bib on him, but he always manages to get ices on himself anyway.

I treasure my nephew and always will. Hashem created children to bring joy and happiness.

Miriam D.

Loyalty

Family means loyalty and commitment. Sometimes an emergency arouses our compassion. We realize the loving and positive attitude that we have for our siblings, especially in a time of need.

This does not mean that you will always be perfectly patient. However, you have to strive to see the positive, to encourage and appreciate your sibling and to accept your sibling as your colleague.

•❖ *Together Again*

It was the second day of Passover. The table was set in its Yom Tov finery. The atmosphere was calm and peaceful. There was a knock at the door. My father walked in—ALONE. My 11 year-old brother was missing! My worst fear had come true. Terror gripped my heart. I picked up a book of Tehillim and started to pray tearfully.

The search began. My parents went to his friends' houses but he wasn't there. They went up and down the block calling his name. He was nowhere to be found. A thunderstorm had begun outside and the lightning pierced the sky. I looked out the window and up at the sky and prayed, "God, please watch over my brother and bring him home quickly!"

About two hours later my brother walked in. He was fine. Of course there was a story, but the bottom line was that he was alright.

The lesson I learned that night will remain with me forever. Every week when my father walks in from the synagogue with my brother behind him I whisper a prayer of thanks. I'm so glad my precious brother is safely home.

Shaindy K.

- Help and encourage your siblings in big and small ways. Work together.
- Express your love and appreciation from time to time.
- Include a younger sibling in different activities.
- Make a sibling feel special.
- Go for a walk with a younger sibling.
- Buy your sibling a treat. A simple treat such as an ice cream can be an encouraging surprise.
- Say thank you.
- Remember that no one will stand by you your whole life the way your siblings will.

Siblings Are Forever

A cool spring breeze whispered gently as Miriam and I made our way home after a long day at school. We were strolling leisurely down 16th Avenue, discussing the events of our day in the busy world of Bais Yaakov High School.

"Tests, test, tests and more tests," Miriam complained. "We had Math yesterday, Literature today and there's Chemistry tomorrow. Soon my brain will explode."

"What test did you say we were having tomorrow?"

"Chemistry. Why do you look so surprised?"

"I forgot about it. I don't have any notes. What will I do?"

Miriam offered to let me photocopy her notes. I rummaged in my pockets. I found many things but no money. I checked my loose-leaf, my shirt pocket and my pencil case. Miriam checked too. We had no money. Suddenly I heard someone call my name. I turned around and saw my sister standing nearby.

"Why are you congregating at the door?" she asked. "Do you need anything?"

"Yes, you're the perfect person. Do you have any money?"

My sister smiled and whipped out a fresh, crisp dollar bill. Hashem sent my sister in my time of need. My sister has "saved" me more than once. What would I do without my big sister?

P.S. I got 100% on my chemistry test.

Devora E.

When you want to thank people for something they've done right, it's great to tell them, but even greater if you tell them in front of other people. When we say our thanks publicly people know we really mean it.

Saying thank you is a vital principle. We have already set aside time to thank Hashem each day and record Hashem's gifts to us.

Family and Friends

What if we had a time set aside for thanking our family and friends? Occasionally you might do more than just talk. You might give a memento of your recognition, like a card or a small gift. It's not the cost that counts. It's the time you took to single out that special someone.

Everyone appreciates a thank you. Recognition doesn't have to be fancy. It can be as effortless as a handwritten note that says, "You helped me so much. You're the best sister one could have. I'm proud of our family."

Needlepoint

Every *Motzaei Shabbos* when I visited my grandmother, I was surprised by the "magic" light that turned on in front of the house as soon as we got out of the car. It felt good to stand on tiptoe and ring the bell. I quickly got into a sideways stance to shove the door open before the buzzer stopped. The door was open. Without turning, I waited for the footsteps of my parents behind me. When they too were at the doorway, I walked into the house.

I climbed a mountain of white steps. I am not sure what I thought about—playing with my cousins, asking my grandmother questions, eating cookies? Sometimes I paused to admire the framed photographs on the stairwells as I ascended. However, I always reached the top step first. My parents followed behind me. There was my grandmother, standing with arms outstretched to welcome me.

We entered the big living room. The windows were covered with heavy hunter green damask draperies. The valance and the draperies were edged in two feet of ecru lace. Three lamps stood on black marble tables. Another mahogany table held a marble chess set. The sofa had deep green flowers on an emerald background. The sofa and the cushions were covered with a vinyl slipcover. Above the sofa there were olive green shutters. The wallpaper felt like velvet. There were tall palms growing in flower pots opposite the piano. Every inch of wall space was covered with needlepoint pictures. The parquet floor was polished and there was a Persian rug in the center. The room smelled faintly of Jean Naté—my grandmother's favorite perfume.

The living room was definitely elegant. Yet, I must confess that as a child I didn't feel as impressed by all of it as by the coffee table near the couch. On the coffee table there was a large plastic tray. My grandmother had set out bittersweet chocolate, potato chips, and homemade sugar cookies. I looked hopefully to my grandmother and waited for an invitation to taste something delicious.

Grandmother was different than any of my friends' grandmothers.

Most grandmothers are old-fashioned, bent and gray. My grandmother was completely different.

Her golden blond wig was short and stylish. Her bright blue eyes glimmered and laughed gaily. She sat erect opposite the couch in her olive green easy chair. On her knees there was an immense needlepoint picture. It had pink and white roses on a gray-blue background. She wore a white dress with a cheerful pattern of navy blue flowers and many navy buttons. I knew the pattern well because after sewing the dress for herself, she made one for me that I proudly wore all summer long. Grandmother was definitely the life of the room. It was as if she were a flowering fruit tree in a forest of evergreens.

Grandmother held out her hand, "Come here my Rosie. You haven't said hello. Do you have time for me? Can we talk a bit before you go to play with your cousins?"

I glanced at the cookies and rushed to her side. I perched on the narrow wooden arm of the easy chair. Grandmother put her arm around me. If she was nervous that I might topple off she didn't show it. "That's better, it's so good to see you." She looked at me warmly. "You are almost ready to be a bride."

I laughed. "I'm only seven-years-old!"

Grandmother held up the needlepoint so that the light of the lamp shone on it. She examined it quietly. "I'm working on a needlepoint and I wanted to hear what you think. "

I felt honored and a bit surprised. My grandmother had never consulted with me about any of her other needlepoint pictures. "I love it. It's beautiful."

Grandmother pointed to the flowers. "Is the color lively enough? I don't want it to be dull."

"Look! It has roses like my name. The flowers are pink. Pink is my favorite color."

"What about the table in the picture?" Grandmother asked.

"It looks like the table right near your chair. All it needs is a lace covering like this one."

Grandmother nodded. Her face expressed nothing. She was concentrating on a secret thought. I waited patiently for two whole minutes but grandmother was just looking at the needlepoint and thinking.

"Your cookies are delicious," I hinted.

Grandmother picked up her thread bag and began to rummage in it. "I made the cookies for you. Please take some and then go to Binyomin. Tell him that I asked him to play checkers with you."

I cheerfully selected several cookies and rushed down the dim hallway. I knew I'd find my big cousin Binyomin in the last room in the back. "Bubby said to play checkers with me," I announced.

Binyomin put down his book with a sigh and a smile and got up to get the magnetic checkers set from the shelf.

I returned every week for conversation, cookies and checkers. Eventually I even learned how to play chess. Grandmother never discussed her picture with me again. I didn't think about it much. I was too busy telling her about everything under the sun.

I talked about my friends. I announced that I would sing in the school choir. The news about my summer in camp was exciting. A year later I was in the camp circus.

There were birthday parties and Chanukah parties. On Purim my cousin played the piano. My grandmother cooked all the food for all the parties and it was always delicious.

Every week we came and every week Grandmother sat in her chair to the right of the doorway. There was always a needlepoint in progress on her lap. There were always cookies on the coffee table. Every week I'd perch on the arm of her chair and tell my proud grandmother what was happening in my life. One week I told her with excitement that I was going to be the head of the elementary school choir.

Several months later we came to visit on Shabbos night but the first easy chair to the right of the doorway was empty. I stood at the doorway and looked around the room. It was full of people. My cousins were there. My aunt and uncle and my parents sat on the low couch. But the easy chair at the doorway was empty and the room was silent.

I saw the pictures on the walls. I noticed the rug on the floor. The windows had their damask curtains. I tried not to look at the coffee table. There was bittersweet chocolate in the candy dish. But of course there were no cookies.

Five years later, I really was a bride. A week before my wedding, I sat and spoke to my mother. I whispered wistfully, "Remember how Bubby always called me her bride. I wish grandmother would have lived to see me get married. "

My mother was quiet. Her face was somber. Her eyes looked at me, but I couldn't tell what she was thinking. Then she surprised me with a smile. With a quick movement she jumped up.

"Come with me."

I followed my mother upstairs. She went to the wardrobe at the far end of her bedroom and opened the top drawer. The top drawer held my mother's miscellaneous personal belongings—birth certificates, old passports, and perhaps letters on creased and yellowed paper. There was silence for a moment.

My mother pulled out a yellowed plastic bag. She opened the snaps at the top of the bag and pulled out a roll of tissue paper. I watched my mother unroll several layers of tissue paper. There was a rolled- up needlepoint canvas.

"What is this?"

My mother handed me the canvas. " I've been saving this for you for a long time. It's yours."

I unrolled the canvas slowly. I saw the gray background and the pink roses in a cobalt vase. The vase was on a table with an ecru lace tablecloth. I held it at arm's length. I had never seen the completed picture before. For a second I just stood looking at it with my mouth open in a circle.

"Grandmother made it for you. She gave it to me when you were thirteen and told me to put it away until your wedding day. "

I looked up at my mother. We were both crying. "It's beautiful!" I whispered.

I sat down on the bed and placed the tapestry on it. I held it and studied it carefully for a while. I felt like the little girl who used to sit on the armchair, curious and absorbed. I turned the tapestry over and glanced at the back. "Look at this! The back is so smooth and perfect. Grandmother was amazing. It's neat and precise without any hanging threads."

I couldn't decide which of the flowers I liked best. Perhaps I favored the pink one. I remembered our earlier conversations about favorite colors. Grandmother had wanted to know what I liked. She was an adult who could make a child feel important. I pictured grandmother sitting in her chair and stitching. Strand by strand, she added to her masterpiece. What did she think of when she carefully chose her colors and shades?

This picture meant so much to me. It was a way to remember Grandmother every day. I would turn to look at her picture on the wall several times each day and remember what's important. Often I would wish that I were more like Grandmother. Once in a while I might succeed. The picture would make me feel good when problems seemed overwhelming.

Grandmother had accomplished something really important. She was no longer alive for my wedding and yet she was here.

Reluctantly, I reached for the tissue paper to protect the picture when I put it away. "You won't need the tissue paper again," my mother said. "I'm taking it to the custom framing store today. In two weeks the picture will be ready for the wall of your new home."

༺༻

Is there any way I can thank my grandmother now for the love she stitched into the needlepoint picture? Her love lasted longer than a lifetime.

One of my grandmother's principles was that family should see each other and do things together often. Don't wait for special occasions. Take the time to visit frequently. Grab a few moments to talk every day. Look for creative ways to share a part of you with others. It may be something as small as homemade cookies or as major as a needlepoint picture.

I can't visit with my grandmother right now. I wish I could hear her speak. There are many things I want to tell her. If you can visit your grandparents, please do and don't put it off for tomorrow.

Wise Words

There are experiences that change our lives. Sometimes the experience changes our family's life. If a lesson is learned, the experience can change many other people's lives too.

Meaningful experiences may be encountered when one is young or old. Regardless of when they occur, important lessons are learned. This contributor will never forget the power of the lesson she learned one year. Instead of being melancholy she decided to change the future. She has come to understand that no matter how young or how old you are you can learn to make a difference.

Don't Wait for Tomorrow

I lost the opportunity of a lifetime! I couldn't believe it. My grandfather had passed away during his sleep. I was assured that he didn't feel any pain, but the guilt tormented me anyway. Any moment, I thought, someone would shout, "She is guilty! She never really got to know her grandfather."

I was never really interested in the stories my grandfather told about his heroic past. Sometimes I'd smile and nod politely, but I never truly comprehended his precious words and the concepts they expressed. Other times, I mumbled an excuse about going out just for a bit of fresh air, but I didn't return to hear those fascinating stories.

Then I realized that I couldn't change the past but I could change the future. Now I look forward to visiting my remaining grandparents. I don't take them for granted. I listen patiently and comment enthusiastically when they reminisce about their lives in prewar Europe. I now have a deeper appreciation of my heritage. My loss made me realize that grandparents are precious and have so much to offer.

❧ A Treasured Mitzvah

I like to visit my grandfather, Moshe Brachfeld. He was born in Poland and he survived all six years of the Holocaust. He escaped from ghetto to ghetto, bunker to bunker and from one concentration camp to the next.

"My brother, Mendel, and I had the special merit of having a pair of tefillin with us throughout most of the war years," he told me.

"This special pair of tefillin was our treasure. We carried them with us wherever we went. Even at night we hid the tefillin in our bed.

"Every day about a hundred men used to line up around us. All these Jews were willing to risk their lives to perform the mitzvah of tefillin. Two men guarded and blocked the man putting on the tefillin so that no one would see him. Each person got either a tefillin shel yad or a tefillin shel rosh. There was no time for everyone to put on both. If we would have been caught, we'd have been put to death instantly.

"This pair of tefillin was our treasure. We went through extreme measures to protect and keep them. We gave up our day's portion of food many times for this special pair of tefillin."

After the war this pair of tefillin disappeared. My father says, "Hashem has a 'museum' with all the mitzvos that Jews endured suffering in order to fulfill."

B. Brachfeld

Bubby, You Are My Sunshine

Looking at the memories our family shares,
You are my sunshine in despair.
Bubby, your encouraging smile
Helped me go the extra mile.

When I smiled you laughed along,
When I sang you harmonized.
When I frowned you cried,
Your pain mirrored mine.

The treasured moments spent together,
In our hearts will remain forever.
Truly one of a kind,
A grandmother like you is hard to find.

Bubby, your cheerful words set things just right,
When I'm in the dark, Bubby brings me light.
Wherever life leads me, whichever way
Our hearts together will always remain.

Yocheved F.

❧ Letter to Your Grandmother

Of course girls care about their grandparents. Somehow, though, they never get around to saying it. They think it doesn't need to be said because everyone knows it already. It's important for children to thank grandparents not only for the gifts they bring but for who they are. This is also true of saying something generous and encouraging.

Teens share the loving letters they have written to their grandparents.

Dear Bubby,

I wish I could see you and Grandpa more often. It was so nice when my family lived just a few houses away from yours. Well, at least when I see you in the summer I really appreciate you.

I enjoy your phone calls to me. You seem to have a way of speaking pleasantly and cheerfully to everyone—friend, acquaintance, Jew and non-Jew. You care for others and treat them all like your child.

Although you have many grandchildren I feel as if I'm your only one. I know everyone loves you and I feel secure in your hands. You make me feel special.

With your awareness of people's problems and willingness to help them you have made a good name for yourself. You have also made a good name for me, your granddaughter.

Thank you Bubby,
C.B. Pepper

Dear Bubby,

It is your past that has built our future. All of your grandchildren are fortunate to have the opportunity to have such a special Bubby. You, my special Bubby, created a royal legacy for me and other fortunate children.

You are the mother of our family. You are strong in your beliefs in a corrupt generation. Your achievements are never ending. You sacrifice your own needs for others again and again. You do so many great things modestly behind the scenes.

I hope you see Yiddish nachas from all of us. May Hashem give you strength, health and prosperity.

Miriam Sigall

Dear Bubby,

Everyone has a bubby but none are like you. I look at my mother and thank Hashem for her loving, caring and giving ways. She has taught me so much about life. I know that my mother learned to be this way from you.

When I visit you I understand how special you were to her when she was growing up. You have so much good advice to give. I wish we could spend more time together so that I could get to know you better. Please, come visit again soon.

Mindy B.

Dear Bubby,

Unfortunately, I did not meet or get to know Zaidy. But you Bubby have kept Zaidy alive. You tell us what Zaidy would do, what Zaidy would have thought. Zaidy is a part of your everyday speech. The stories you tell us about him describe his respect for Torah sages and his devotion to his children, his siblings and all the people in the shul where he was a Rov.

In the process I learn a lot about you too, Bubby. I learn about the common values you both shared. You have given me a sense of pride in who I am. I hope to live my life by your principles and values. Thank you Bubby, for being you.

Love your granddaughter,
Shaindy B.

Dear Bobby,

Bobby, I want to be like you when I grow up. I admire you because you have built a true Jewish family on a foundation of strong Jewish faith.

How did you feel when you came to the shores of America and saw the Statue of Liberty guarding the harbor? You were penniless. You didn't even have family—you were all alone. You were the sole survivor of a thriving family that was slaughtered in the horrifying Holocaust.

You have often told me about that beast called Mengele. He signaled your family to go to the left and for you to go to the right. And as you ran to join them on the left, Mengele slapped you on your cheek and you stayed on the right and survived.

You saw your family walking, holding hands on their way to an unknown destination. Then you looked up and saw pitch black smoke and that's all that remained of your family.

You never gave up hope. You suffered hunger and back-breaking work but you never gave up. You survived not only physically but also spiritually—because you never lost faith in Hashem.

The temptations of America were many for a newly arrived immigrant. Would your life not have been easier if you had worked on Shabbos? However, you decided that the Nazis had taken away everything but they wouldn't take away your religion. You were steady and strong in your beliefs and you have rebuilt a new world on smoldering ashes.

I want to be like you, dear grandmother, when I grow up. I want to be able to look around with satisfaction like you do and say, the sacrifices were many but the rewards are more than I could have possibly imagined.

I admire you, Bobby.

Love,
Malkie S.

༄

Dear Bubby,

Many people look at the world and see it in different ways. You always see the good in everything while others see the bad. You always encourage me and say, "Something good will come out of this."

I think you will always be cheerful. You never give up hope even when others would give up right away.

Your granddaughter,
Yehudis G.

Sharing a Good Deed

In the beginning we may think our options are limited. The dream of involving your family in a united act of kindness may seem distant. How will you express your dream? How will you convince others to become involved in this pursuit? It seems impossible, impractical and inconceivable.

When you read the examples below you will probably admire the families involved. You may think it's marvelous. Perhaps you will sigh and say, "Maybe next year." This is the usual response. Then wistful looks appear.

Everyone enjoys reading about consequential acts of consideration. After you spend some time together with the teens and their families in the stories, I hope you will decide to act. A sense of exuberance bonds the family that does mitzvos together. There are smiles and peaceful, happy faces. Acts of kindness give our lives power and significance. So ask yourself the question—if these families did this positive act together, what can my family do?

Exercise

Is there a good deed that you have done together with your family or your friends? How did that make it more meaningful?

_____
_____

What good deeds would you like to do with others in the future? Write them down even if you aren't sure how you will accomplish them.

_____
_____

If you woke up tomorrow and were already a parent with children of your own, what would you want your family to accomplish?

_____
_____

The First Time

Do you have a ready smile? Do you believe that people are basically good? Are you sensitive to their emotions? Do you notice problems that need to be tackled? Do you have strong convictions? Can you share knowledge without making others feel stupid? Do people feel good around you? Are you interested in learning from others?

If you can answer yes to these questions, you are ready to start sharing good deeds more often.

You have a bigger impact than you think you do. And everyone gains. Everyone gets ahead. It really is like that.

Sharing a good deed is the best investment in the world because the benefits just grow and grow. Don't be afraid to share your life. Often you will find that when you share a mitzva with others you gain a deeper perspective. You begin to realize the significance of your ordinary actions.

How many times have you selected a cookie, mumbled the appropriate blessing and popped it into your mouth? Most of us probably say one hundred blessings each day. We know that in order to eat the cookie we have to say nine words. When we are in a hurry we forget to allow each of those words to penetrate. Leah discovered an entirely new way of looking at the blessings we say from the group of students she tutors every week.

·∞·

I tutor a group of immigrants who recently arrived from Russia. On the last day of the first term, I gave out cookies. I said a blessing with each person when I handed her the cookie. I felt self-conscious because some students looked at me in a surprised way.

One student started crying as she said the blessing. Every syllable of the blessing was something important to her. With tear-filled eyes she said, "We didn't know. No one taught us. The communists didn't let us learn." I was stunned that a simple thing I did brought such a stirring response. I feel like crying now as I tell you about it. We take our blessings for granted, but I learned from this to have a deeper awareness and appreciation.

Observing her students started her thinking. She asked herself—"How can I put more feeling into the blessings I say each day?" Leah also realized that hidden in all of her students is a deep desire to know their Jewish heritage. She resolved to find practical ways to share other mitzvos.

When Rina heard Leah's story she added, "A 22-year-old Russian boy is staying at my neighbor's house. He just had a Bris Milah and he's recuperating at their house. He wants to learn about his Jewish heritage. His family doesn't know he did it."

∞

I'll never forget the day I handed the babysitter who works for us an esrog and lulav and recited the blessing slowly with her. She was intrigued by the esrog and examined it with curiosity and surprise. Although she was at least 60 years old she had never said the blessing on the esrog and lulav before. She paid attention to each word I said and with emotion in her trembling voice repeated the holy words after me. I will always remember the emotion of the moment. It seemed that her heart was on fire. I had just said the same words a few moments earlier, yet my babysitter's blessing seemed more real. Perhaps it was her simple faith—she knew Hashem was listening. She felt His presence right there.

Throughout the day there was an unexplained bounce in my step. I thought about that pure blessing. How can I describe the radiant expression I had seen on the wrinkled, care-worn face? Perhaps I had looked like that on my wedding day.

Every person can make a difference. Miracles are waiting to happen every day. We can help those who never had the opportunity to finally learn and connect. Together, goals can be reached that no one imagined. The power of the first time can't be measured.

Family and Friends ☐ 129

Perhaps you will hear about the results from that initial blessing, but probably you won't. Yet once a heart is set on fire delicious, wonderful developments occur. Don't be shy about sharing your blessings. As the saying goes, "Hey, you never know!

A Joyful Heart

*P*eace descends upon the earth. I glance out the window and stare in wonder as the fiery sun is about to set. Its golden rays reflect upon the hilltops. My mother lights the candles with a fervent prayer upon her lips. The daily rush, the coming and going of commercial life, is gone. Taking its place is the rush of religious Jews hurrying to shul to daven. I glance at the glowing Shabbos candles reflected on the snow white tablecloth, amidst glittering silverware and china. My heart wants to jump as joy fills me.

The family sits around the Shabbos table as the candles cast a warm glow, and the aroma of delicious food wafts through the air. The Kiddush is recited, and the meal is served. Filled with yearning, my father begins singing zemiros. He leans forward with a concentrated look on his face as he begins a melody. My brothers join in, giving the melody renewed fervor with their eager, powerful voices. My younger siblings sing along with their clear sweet voices completing the harmony.

The melody envelops us all. As the melody ends our faces are radiant. The meal continues, with anxieties of the week banished from our thoughts.

As my weary head contentedly touches my pillow, I ponder happily, "Shabbos is the sign of a Jew. It adds beauty to our existence. It gives us a realistic feeling of spirituality!"

Tziri G.

Memorable Moments

There are some moments that we will always remember. These moments seem ordinary enough at the time but when we look back now and think about everything that developed since then, we realize that these moment were crucial. It takes a moment to say "yes" to a remarkable opportunity. It also takes a moment to say "no." Our answer can make all the difference.

How many times does the phone ring on a busy day? What will happen when we pick up the receiver? Usually our phone call is simply a mundane conversation. We talk for a few minutes and continue what we were doing before the phone rang. Sometimes the phone call requires a response. We are faced with a decision. We might respond by extending ourselves and calmly going to work. There are times when one will whisper the simple words, "Yes, I'm here to help," and save a life. Pessy's father heard the phone ring and went to answer. That phone call was just the beginning.

"It all began with a phone call." Pessy said. When Pessy's father realized there was an emergency he immediately began to help. Becoming involved gave her family many gifts.

- They were able to make a big difference every day.
- They all worked together.
- Each person was making a significant contribution.
- They felt satisfaction as they encouraged their relatives.
- Boruch Hashem they celebrated together when their cousin was once again happy and healthy.

•◦ *Hospitality*

It all started early one morning. I heard a joyous "Mazel Tov," but then my father's voice changed to a concerned tone. When my father hung up the phone he told us that a relative in Israel had given birth to a baby boy with a hole in his heart. The family was extremely concerned because they had spoken to the top doctors in Israel about the operation. Many doctors had performed the operation but none had ever succeeded.

Our family called up hospitals all over the world to see who could perform this operation. The choices finally narrowed down to two top hospitals—one in Geneva and one in Manhattan.

We asked our relatives if the baby could have the operation in Manhattan so they could stay with us. They arrived on a special plane. They didn't know what to do first. We took the baby to the hospital and then brought the family to our house. Over the next few weeks everyone in my family helped them with whatever they needed.

The baby underwent a very successful operation, thank God, and the doctors fully repaired his heart. When my relatives went back to Israel they couldn't stop thanking us. They said that they didn't know how they would have managed without us.

A few months later we received pictures of the baby in the mail. It was gratifying to see the happy and healthy boy smiling at us in the picture. My whole family was happy we were able to help.

Pessy K.

A Mother and Daughter Together

Our resolutions on Rosh Hashanah almost never produce lasting change. In fact, we sometimes feel uncomfortable to be regretting the same mistakes as last year, don't we? Perhaps you've resolved to improve in the mitzvah of honoring parents. Here is an exercise that will be helpful in preparing you for a fresh start. Proceed at a gentle pace.

Take a deep breath, relax and fill in this sentence with the first thought that comes to your mind.

In my opinion, the reason most Rosh Hashanah resolutions do not last is because:

And because:

Other thoughts:

In my opinion, the reason the resolution to improve in the area of honoring parents doesn't last is because:
We have many stresses and we are so busy that we put off doing anything about our resolution.

And because:
We don't realize that the small considerate acts we do every day make a big difference.

⁂

Would you rather receive a gift you really wanted, or give your mother a gift she would absolutely treasure? Take some times to do a mitzvah together with your mother and you will be receiving and giving simultaneously. Perhaps you will begin a tradition that you will sustain and maintain week after week. Chany shares her experience:

> When I was young I began lighting a Shabbos candle right next to my mother's big candelabra. Those enchanted moments are still close to my heart today. As my mother lit the big silver candelabra I imitated all her motions and repeated the words of the blessing after her. I then closed my eyes and swayed back and forth. My mother said that it was a good time to ask God for anything I wanted. At that time in my young life I wished for candy, gum and lots of ice cream.
>
> What I remember many years later was the togetherness that I felt with my mother. There wasn't any other time when I felt quite the same feeling. It was only that once a week event. I have never forgotten it.
>
> *Chany T.*

> I loved my little tin Menorah. I picked those colorful wax candles so carefully. I set up everything hours before the actual candle lighting on Chanukah night.
>
> I stood close to my father and followed his every move. When he began reciting the blessing I slowly repeated every word. I took my father's candle and watched my thin bright candles start to burn. Joy swelled within me. I was like an adult now.
>
> The images of those Chanukah lights when I was much younger are warmly remembered. I'll never forget them.
>
> *Chaya Sara Gluck*

Delivering Kindness

Shaindy describes how one thoughtful gesture led to a wonderful journey for her family. Their family began filling their lives to the brim with acts of kindness.

My mother noticed some neighbors who lived with the bare necessities. She arranged to have a brother-in-law pick up some cakes and challahs and whatever could be spared from a neighborhood bakery.

A week later, on his way home, my father noticed a tremendous bag of bagels and rolls laying out on the curb waiting to be picked up by a garbage truck. He arranged with the bakery's owner to have all the extra bakery goods donated to poor large families. The owner is an extraordinary person. He delivered the extra goods to our home each night. Each family member went to distribute these breads and cakes to those in need so that they would have the bakery goods ready for breakfast the next morning.

My aunt divided the Thursday night delivery. My mother sent each of my bothers to a different family with a package.

My brothers were 11 and 13. They were shy and embarrassed to go to families they didn't know and give them these bags. My mother convinced them that the mitzvah is greater than their embarrassment. At first they did it reluctantly but then it became a habit every Friday and before each holiday.

My brothers actually took over the responsibility of knowing to whom to bring the packages. They developed a close relationship with these families. When the children saw my brothers at the door they exclaimed with joy and laughter. They knew that there were goodies for them in those bags. We have even shared celebrations with these families.

After a few years, my oldest brother was leaving to study in Israel. He told the mother of the family that his younger brother will continue in his place. We have kept up this mitzvah every week, with joy and happiness on both ends.

Shaindy L.

Benefits of Reaching Out

BENEFIT ONE: You uncover talents and strengths you never knew you had.

BENEFIT TWO: You learn new skills.

BENEFIT THREE: You meet people who appreciate the real you.

BENEFIT FOUR: You become one of those rare people who has a sense of purpose.

BENEFIT FIVE: Once you begin making kindness a habit, you will find that you have more energy and you can do more than you expected.

Caring and Sharing

- Can the simple things you do bring happiness to others?
- Are you afraid to be you?
- Do you acquire satisfaction when you give to others?

Some Concepts to Consider:

- We are born with the courage to approach others and share.
- A quick and easy way to acquire satisfaction is to do someone a favor.
- When you make someone else happy you feel happier with yourself.
- We can bring happiness to others by doing something simple that shows we care.

Our family helps an elderly couple in my building with whatever they need. Rabbi R. has asthma attacks. He was rushed to the hospital quite a few times already. His wife was in a car accident and had a slow recovery. Last year during the blizzard I insisted on going shopping for them. It was only one block away but I came back half an hour later and I was freezing. You don't know how happy I made her. Every Shabbos we go to visit and it makes her Shabbos more enjoyable. It's not just that you help a person. You are showing them that you care about them and that makes them feel much happier.

C.G.R.

In the summer, two women knocked on the door of our bungalow. They were collecting for a poor bride. They were strangers in the bungalow colony. My mother realized that they needed someone to help them get around the large colony.

My mother and a few other women agreed to join them. The results were outstanding. They collected more than they had originally hoped to gather. My mother told me she was happy to help even though she didn't know the bride for whom they had collected.

M.F.

Together In Mitzvos

Our entire family always comes together to do the mitzvah of Tashlich. During Aseres Yemei Teshuvah, we go to the water near a local Toys R Us with our prayer books and our bag of challah pieces. We pray for a good and healthy new year and throw our challah into the river. I think about how throwing the challah into the water symbolizes throwing away our sins and I pray to God to become a new pure person.

I remember that Tashlich was such a fun thing to do when I was a child. This is terrific—you throw away your sins and then go to Toys R Us for a new toy. It was a blast!

Now I understand that this mitzvah is also very special. It is a time when every member of the family appears with a prayer book in one hand and a bag of challah in the other. Even my married siblings come with their spouses and their children. Last year my young nephew sang a song about Tashlich. He was adorable.

It feels good to know that at a time when we are praying for so many precious things, we are all praying together as a family. Every one of us is together in a special spiritual endeavor.

Leah B.

Every Friday night during the meal we take out a halachah sefer and take turns reading some halachos. Some are easy and others are more complex. It is a spiritual thing and afterwards our conversation is different. There is a special feeling in the air.

Shira Y. Maler

*W*hen I was visiting in the nursing home I met a cheerful elderly lady. She told me about her good years in Germany before the War. Then she told me about all her grandchildren. "I guess they are busy with their own friends and they don't understand how it feels to be in a nursing home all alone seeing old faces. I wouldn't mind seeing them once in a while." My heart went out to her. Please, if you have a grandmother or someone you know who is all alone, go visit them. It may be boring in the beginning, but in the end—you'll realize how many interesting things they have to say about life in Europe or life here in America. Life was so different then. Try it! From my experience I can say that I really do enjoy visiting and learning from their experiences.

Bayla Sima S.

Friends

What Is a True Friend?

     A smile.
A reassuring word.
That's what makes the difference.

     A lending hand.
     A shoulder to cry on.
     A good influence.
That's what makes a good friend.

An encouraging word when it's needed most.
A welcoming, shining face popping up unexpectedly when you feel you need a pal
     To be there with you.

A person who is fortunate to have friends,
Does not know absolute sadness.

A beacon of light in the seemingly endless tunnel
Of decisions, mistakes and pressure
Of adolescence.

An honest opinion.
A shopping escort.
Someone to help you finish that endless ice cream sundae.

     ....A true friend.

Gitty Skolnick

There's a part of each person that wants to establish connections. We want to understand others and be understood. We want to listen to others and have others lend an ear to us. We yearn to connect with our classmates. Perhaps we are sitting and waiting for the phone to ring. Everyone is waiting for an invitation. "Why didn't she call?" a voice asks inside us. On the other hand, "Why not make the first move?"

Did someone pass by in the hall and casually pay you a compliment? Trust the compliment. Give yourself a moment to let the compliment echo and grow. Be sincere when you acknowledge the person speaking to you and focus on her. How can you return the compliment? Can you say something meaningful along with the usual "Thank you"? Don't just receive compliments, pass them on. Look around you. Is there someone new with whom you can connect? Think of something encouraging that you can tell them although you don't yet know them well.

You can make a new friend any time you want to — even today. What are some good ways to make a friend? List some ideas here. Then try one of them. Write what happens.

_____

_____

_____

_____

_____

_____

_____

_____

_____

_____

_____

A Special Friend

What is a friendly attitude? Is it a willingness to like me as I am? Is it appreciation for any small kindness I might offer? Perhaps it's listening to me and making me feel that what I say is fascinating. A friend makes you feel happy and comfortable. Sometimes a friend will cheer you up when life seems overwhelming.

Esther is one ordinary girl with an extraordinarily friendly attitude. She has helped one small seven-year-old by doing something to make his life better. She didn't know where this would lead. She simply continued in various small ways to make her neighbor feel welcome. Esther decided to do what she could. She didn't tell Dovid he was different. She overlooked the fact that he couldn't do things as well as other children. It's true that abilities that come naturally to so many others don't come naturally to Dovid. Esther related to me, however, that Dovid has a unique advantage. He's a magnificent friend.

> *People look at Dovid queerly, but I look at him with love. He is a special child. I met Dovid for the first time on the day I moved to Bayswater. We lived across the road. He ran across the street and right through our front door to show us a toy. We didn't know what hit us. We felt slightly frightened and intruded upon.*
>
> *As time passed, I realized that there are things I could learn from Dovid. He has problems, yet he always wears a smile. I have never heard him complain. He goes to a special non-Jewish school, but he eagerly learns with a Rebbe in his spare time. Would I have his inner strength if I were in his shoes?*
>
> *I frequently invite him over to our house. He is absolutely ecstatic if I spend fifteen minutes talking to him, and he loves the simplest story I tell him. He's extremely grateful for any small thing I give him. I enjoy giving Dovid things and watching his face light up. He's really appreciative and enjoys life's simple pleasures.*
>
> *Dovid is a special child and I love him.*
>
> *Esther F.*

The Perfect Present

I just wanted to tell you
That I still have the compliment you gave me.
It's in a very private place
And when I'm depressed
I pull it out and gaze at it.
I look at it from all angles,
Take it apart and rearrange it,
And it still works.
Thanks again.
It was a perfect present.

This poem shows the power of a compliment. When people give a compliment they have no idea what it may mean to the other person. It can change someone completely. For example, I know someone who had an old short coat. She wore it as a jacket. She was slightly embarrassed about it, because the inside was worn and it was missing a button.

One day her friend asked, "Oh! Did you get your coat in _____?" — she mentioned an exclusive store. The wearer felt so good that now she wears her coat every day and loves it.

The next time you want to say something, think! Will I raise someone up or knock her down?

Malka G.

The Power of a Smile

Smiling is a simple yet potent act. A smile is a healing force. A tiny infant recognizes a smile and he smiles and laughs back at you. When one looks at the baby with a somber expression the child may begin to cry. A smile affects everyone. It can help you feel better physically and emotionally. It propels you to think positive thoughts and generates restorative forces in your brain. A 16th century sage asserted that people who smile will stay younger longer.

A smile helps friendships begin. It also is the sunshine of our relationships. Everyone is waiting for your smile.

✢ *Smile!*

A smile—
A gentle curve slanting upwards
Bringing joy, hope, trust and friendship.
A smile—
Showing caring, loving kindness,
Brightening a gloomy day,
Making a world of a difference.

A frown—
A firm curve
Slanting downwards, showing disapproval.
Voicing criticism,
Throwing a black cloud over a bright sun.

We—
We have the power
To bring—
To bring joy,
Or
To dispel it
With a single expression.

Rifky Spitzer

Just Be Yourself

A lot of us feel that if we could just be a little more like someone else we would be popular, pretty and smart. We imagine that our friends have it all. We try to compete by buying just the right skirt, or the newest pair of shoes. In spite of our best efforts we feel a longing, a hole inside us that can't be filled. We don't know why.

You are special. You have intrinsic worth, and you are a good person. Knowing this is the foundation of your growth.

Sometimes we doom ourselves to failure because we have unrealistic ambitions. We continually criticize ourselves because we have taken on more than we can realistically handle, and because we expect ourselves to be someone we aren't. Most people leave school with wonderful fantasies about the perfect lives they will lead, and when the real world doesn't measure up, they blame themselves. But these assumed inadequacies are only in their minds.

Let me tell you about Esty. The first time I met her, she was holding a microphone and announcing the grand prize for the raffles at the annual tea of a national women's organization. You could hear the enthusiasm and friendliness in her voice, and she spoke as though she were in her own living room. The three hundred women in the room did not prevent Esty from being herself.

I asked Esty if she had any particular philosophy that gave her the ability to appear so much at ease in public. Her answer displayed a healthy and realistic attitude toward being human. She told me that she worked constantly at smoothing out her own rough edges, but at the same time she accepted not being perfect. "That's part of the territory," she said.

Even Esty's home reflected her matter-of-fact outlook on life. The house was very pleasant and well-kept, but many of the kitchen fixtures had been purchased second-hand. Esty had had to choose between a brand-new kitchen and putting in a laundry room, and she opted for the latter because it was functional and would make her day-to-day life more convenient. Esty did not berate herself about the impression her second-hand kitchen would make on others, any more than she berated herself for not being perfect; to her, a functional house was more important than impressions. She accepted things as they were.

Esty continued with some important advice: "Don't measure yourself against other people. Don't carry a ruler in your head. Sometimes you go to a wedding or a Bar Mitzvah, and as soon as you enter the room you begin to measure: 'Is my dress too dressy or too casual? Is someone else wearing the same thing? Are my shoes right?' Well, these comparisons are not helpful."

Esty's ideas made me realize how often I had let this quiet voice inside me undermine my own serenity. I discovered that I was not alone. Many people carry an imaginary measuring stick in their minds, and sometimes the "stick" is on duty all day long. It is this stick that makes us run to clean up the house when unexpected visitors are about to show up, because we are sure the house will reflect poorly on us. It is the stick that makes us feel self-conscious when we come in late, convinced that everyone is staring at us and thinking about what a *shlemazel* we are. And it is this same stick that makes us try to find out how everyone else did on last year's final exam.

In order to give up these comparisons, it is essential to understand that Hashem intended everyone to be different. He did not want you to be exactly like the girl who lives next door. In fact, you are so unique that there will never be a person in history who is just like you.

⁂

In the *Alei Shur*, Rav Shlomo Wolbe says that each person has been given the individual tools to fulfill his very individual mission:

> *Each morning in the blessing Sheoso Li Kol Tzorchi we thank God for granting us everything we need to serve Him. We are*

prepared to accomplish our life's tasks... Hashem doesn't want everyone to look at life in the same way and to learn and comprehend identically.

Rav Wolbe illustrates his point with the following story:

> Rav Naftali Amsterdam once said to his rebbe, Rav Yisrael Salanter: "If only I had the head of the Shaagas Arye, the heart of the Yesod Veshoresh HoAvodah, and the great character of Rav Yisrael Salanter. Then I would be able to serve Hashem."
>
> Rav Yisrael answered him: "Naftali, with your mind and your heart and your character, you can also be a true servant of Hashem."

"This is what we have to know," concludes Rav Wolbe. "There will never be another person in history, born in this place to these particular parents, with this unique combination of talents. We must serve Hashem with our mind and our heart and our abilities. There will never be another you."

Are You an Introvert or an Extrovert?

I stood and watched the nursery class. A little girl in a blue dress grabbed a toy and approached her classmate with a smile. Her classmate with the yellow blond hair shook her head and turned back to the book she had been "reading." You have probably met people who are outgoing as well as people who are shy. Psychologists have a specific term for each type of person. The outgoing people are called extroverts and the quiet people are called introverts.

Extroverts excite our imagination. Many of us wait silently in the corner of the room for an extrovert to approach us. We hope that one day the perfect friend will simply say hello and break the ice. Novels tell wonderful stories of people who have met the perfect friend just when they needed them the most. Groups of smiling faces on billboards and magazine advertisements make it seem that we should all be seeking excitement and entertainment.

The extrovert may have many friends and do things in a large group. On the other hand, the introvert may have more success with developing a meaningful relationship. Someone who is quiet and is a good listener will have the patience to build a deep and lasting friendship. An introvert may have just a few friends, yet that small group will remain loyal to each other for years.

Is it better to be an introvert or an extrovert? Is it better to work on your own or to do things with a group? Neither! Our world needs **both** types of people. It needs people who are in between as well.

Read these pairs of statements. Which one sounds most like you? Check A or B for each one.

1. A. I am not easily bored when I'm sitting in one spot.
   B. I am easily bored sitting in one spot.
2. A. I dread amusement parks and fast, scary rides.

B. I love amusement parks and the roller coaster is my favorite ride.

3. A. I would rather celebrate my birthday quietly with a few friends.
   B. I would rather celebrate my birthday at a large party with lots of people.

4. A. I enjoy a quiet Sunday afternoon alone at home.
   B. I always make plans for Sunday afternoons to do something specific with my friends.

5. A. I like to have a few close friends.
   B. I like to have many casual acquaintances.

6. A. I probably would not consider a new sleep-away camp.
   B. I would be interested in going to a new camp.

7. A. I enjoy talking about my outlook on life.
   B. I would rather *do* something than have a discussion.

8. A. I avoid crowded malls.
   B. I like crowded malls.

9. A. If my school made a performance I'd want to work behind the scenes.
   B. If my school made a performance I'd want to be on stage.

10. A. I usually don't say hello to people I don't know.
    B. I enjoy saying hello to lonely people as I walk down the street.

Total Your A's and B's.

Seven or more A's mean you may be an introvert. You may feel more comfortable when you aren't in social situations.

Seven or more B's mean that you may be an extrovert. You're happiest when you are with many other people.

If your result is about the same number of A's and B's, you probably feel comfortable in both situations—with people or alone.

The Opposite of Peer Pressure

Peer Pressure. Pressure denotes a strain or a burden. There is this urgency to be like others. You move with the group. Everyone is doing it so you do it too. Sometimes you even do things against your better judgment. But who is "everyone"?

A small nucleus of a few domineering girls is in the lead. They are the in-crowd. Unfortunately, the in-crowd denotes that an out-crowd exists too. There is also a large group that is in the middle. These are girls who have friends of their own and are quite trendy. They know that the system is unjust but they don't feel they have the leverage to change things.

Does peer pressure signify togetherness? Is it the opposite of unity? Doesn't it tear down friendship and unity? Every day someone's feelings are hurt for a petty reason. The invisible injury and bruises occur inside and are often impossible to repair.

Peer pressure doesn't help anyone get ahead. A girl may be shunned because she lacks talent, isn't adept at dodging a ball or weighs ten pounds too much. A girl may be ignored because her clothes are different. Is it true that things cannot be different?

Here is a story that drew my attention. It is moving and unforgettable. It happened to ordinary tenth graders. It's compelling evidence that caring, sensitivity and harmony are within our reach.

It promised to be a super summer. My fellow counselors and I enthusiastically moved into the bungalow colony and unpacked our belongings. Then something happened that changed everything.

It was the 17th of Tamuz, just two days after we had arrived. My friend innocently plugged in the small tape recorder to hear an inspiring tape, when out of the wall shot red, fiery sparks! Before long the entire bungalow was ablaze. Huge flames poured out of every window and continued to spread wildly, as did the frightening news. We were ten counselors sitting outside at the picnic table. We watched, dumbfounded, as the flames consumed everything we owned.

It was at least twenty minutes before the fire was finally extinguished. We began to walk around looking ghastly to put it mildly, while everyone around us showered us with soothing words and forced food down our dry throats.

The reality began to penetrate. We were left without a single possession! It was the strangest feeling in the world. We had nothing, beside the clothes we were wearing!

That night as I paced up and down my married sister's bungalow I thought a lot about what had happened and why. It made me realize how powerless we really are in this world. Just a few hours ago, I had so much, and now it was all gone! The thought was mind boggling! "We simply have no control over what happens and the things we have, and the things we don't have," I told myself.

After a sleepless night and a weekend spent in a daze, I returned, like the rest of the counselors, to resume life in a newly arranged bungalow, with the few possessions we had each managed to attain. But along with those changes I noticed a change in me and in the rest of the counselors. We began to appreciate every skirt, every pair of shoes and every brush we owned. No gift was too small.

We shared the little we had, until we each had enough of our own. Some of us had more and some less, but we were careful not to arouse any feelings of jealousy.

With each passing day, I realized how fortunate we were to have gone through this big trial. It made us better people. The summer was more than just a super summer. It made each of us grow—together.

E.H.

Their bungalow went up in flames. Everything they owned no longer existed. Their possessions were destroyed. However, a new reality grew out of the ashes. The spark that destroyed their clothes and belongings generated a precious spark within.

They faced a new reality. They derived the strength to cope in their new stark surroundings by being true friends to each other. Until everyone acquired the simple necessities of day-to-day life, they shared the little they had. They rose beyond common pettiness and competition. They were mature and sensitive to each other's feelings. They were sympathetic. Their friend's problem wasn't someone else's—it was their own. This friendship was far more valuable than material possessions.

Their loss brought them together. Instead of competing they endeavored to help. Instead of their goal being to have more, their goal was to be more. They didn't gather possessions, they gave things away. As E.H. said, "The summer was more than just a super summer. It made each of us grow together."

❧ *A Real Friend*

A real friend doesn't migrate in cold weather. I learned this when it was I who needed a friend.

On the day of the graduation trip, I wasn't feeling well. I was in a daze of pain and agony. I walked around trying to keep up with my class. I felt like my world was caving in, but there was one ray of hope and light.

Only one girl came to my aid and commiserated with my pain. She helped me when I needed it. She was the only one who slowed down when I was in pain. She helped me in my time of need. She is a real friend. I still remember her kindness to me and now we have a lasting friendship.

Sarah R. K.

Encourage Others

"*When I was young, I learned that it was a great accomplishment to write an original Torah thought. Now I see that it is a great accomplishment to make an elderly widow happy.*"

(Rav Chaim Ozer in a conversation with Rabbi Mendel Zaks).

Rabbi Miller explains that one of the special acts of kindness of Hashem is that Hashem encourages the humble.

A woman who lives in my neighborhood was diagnosed early and she had to go for weekly treatments. Twice a week a friend took her to Manhattan for the treatments. The treatments nauseated and weakened her. She was in pain and had no appetite.

I remember going to bring supper for her family. I smiled and said, "You look good." I remember her face lit up with happiness as she said, "Thank you." I learned that a smile makes a world of a difference and it takes so very little effort.

Shaindy F.

This year I accomplished something that I had wanted to fulfill very much as I went through the years in school. I befriended a girl who wasn't generally included and rarely socialized with girls her own age. I can say that with God's help I have built up her confidence and she is now accepted and socializing more. Many a time, when one thinks that they are being kind to another person, they are pleasantly surprised. They gain from the kindness as well. This is true for me in several ways.

Shavy W.

*T*here was a girl in camp whose hand and foot were crooked. Many girls stayed away from her and I saw her secluded in a corner. I started to be friendly. Many girls followed my example. Now everyone could see what she was really like inside. When I see her on the street we smile at each other. I'm happy that she's my friend.

Ruchie F.

"*C*haya" came from a broken home. Her father was killed in an accident and her mother was ill. She came to America alone. Finally she got engaged. She was very happy but there was a problem. Who would buy her everything she needed to start a new home? A group of us got together and bought her all the necessary things. We made her a shower and decorated the room and displayed everything beautifully. Her joy and appreciation were tremendous. Since she had been in America for only a short while, she had only a few friends. Many girls decided to dress up and go to her wedding to make her very happy on her wedding day. As a result, she had a happy and exciting day, one she will never forget. We felt wonderful as well, seeing how happy we had made her.

Frady W.

*W*hen my sister was in the hospital with a bad burn a famous singer came and entertained her. She was able to forget her tremendous pain and was actually cheerful. This man took time out of his busy schedule just to make my sister happy. He regularly visits sick children and cheers them up.

Malky P.

Finish the Sentence

Don't worry about the perfect answer. Simply finish the sentence with the first thought that pops up in your mind. This is a quick and easy way to discover helpful ideas about yourself and your friends.

1. I handled someone well when _____.

2. My friend and I enjoy _____.

3. I had fun talking to _____.

4. Someone helped me discover _____.

5. I helped my friend _____.

6. I feel certain about _____.

7. I met _____ after a long time and _____ _____.

8. I think _____ is remarkable because _____ _____.

9. Someone said I look like _____ and _____ _____.

10. I feel happy for _____ because _____.

11. I was surprised when _____.

12. I tried to save _____.

13. I want to send _____ a letter and tell her _____.

14. I played a game with _____. It was fun because
_____.

15. When I was young, my friend and I _____
_____.

16. I miss _____ because _____.

17. I'll always remember when my friend said, _____
_____.

18. I watched the sunrise with _____ and _____
_____.

19. I felt fortunate when _____.

20. I organized a _____ with _____ and
_____.

21. I remember having fun sitting together with _____
because _____.

22. I gave _____ a compliment and she _____
_____.

Family and Friends ☐ 159

A Friend to Everyone

Every day after we eat and recite the *Bentching* (Grace after Meals), we ask Hashem that we should not ever need a gift from another person. We shouldn't be faced with the embarrassment of having someone help us because they feel pity even though they perhaps don't want to lend a hand. Hopefully, we will never need a visit from someone who constantly looks at her watch and sighs at how much of her time we are taking. It can feel uncomfortable to wait when you ask for help. Those moments of hesitation feel like an eternity.

However, there are precious people who become your friend instantly *although* they never met you before. They look for opportunities to care for others. These wonderful instant friends notice what you need and beg you to accept. They feel happy to do more than you asked for and look for small ways to comfort and nurture. They help with a beautiful attitude. These friends are modest and unassuming. They make it seem like they are having fun while extending a helping hand. These people have made it their business to be a friend to everyone.

At 8:00 A.M. her phones start ringing non-stop. At this early hour she gets busy organizing Bikur Cholim rides. She doesn't only organize the rides, she drives people to the hospital as well.

Someone told me that they met her at her home one morning because they needed a ride to Mount Sinai Hospital. She took a look at her passenger and said, "Where is your lunch?"

The passenger said, "Who can think of food at a time like this? Someone in my family is in the hospital."

"You must have lunch," my aunt insisted.

She pulled out a pretty bag and began filling it with food. She put in several clementines, a package of crackers and two bags of potato chips. Afterwards she packed a salad in a container and some cookies in a zip-lock bag. She even found a drink box. This person told me, "There was enough food there not only for me but for everyone who came to visit that day."

Driving people to hospitals isn't the only thing that makes her a terrific person. She has a nice size house and she has put it to good use. Unfortunately, there are many families that come from Israel with sick mothers, fathers or children. My aunt welcomes these people to stay in her basement or even in an empty bedroom.

A family of four came from Eretz Yisrael. The mother had kidney failure. They stayed at my aunt's house for a long time. Boruch Hashem they found a donor for a kidney transplant and raised the necessary funds. The mother eventually recovered and returned to Israel with her family to live a normal life once again.

These are just some of the astounding stories about my aunt and her kindness. There is a long list of her great deeds. May she receive a great reward.

Rechy K.

Rechy's aunt is a friend to everyone. People feel that they've known her for twenty years even at their first meeting. When they are with her they feel encouraged and comforted. Her cheerful nurturing is a source of strength. It makes one's worries dim because they are no longer alone. Her warm smile makes every undertaking seem easy. Her magnetic personality makes you feel good about accepting her thoughtful acts of caring.

Appreciate Our Differences

Excessive demands can make us feel distant when we'd like to be close. Appreciation brings people together. A young child will say thank you for small treats such as a lollipop, an ice cream or some stickers. When we get older it's important to continue to feel truly grateful. Often, instead, we are too busy wondering how to convince someone to give us yet another something that we absolutely must have.

Appreciate simple things—the beautiful trees in the fall, the snow covered rooftops in winter, the clear air after a rain. Notice and feel grateful for the beauty around you. Don't feel too shy to recognize the simple things that people do for you. Say thank you for compliments, small favors, breakfast and lunch that's waiting for you and even your clothes that magically appear in your closet, clean and freshly ironed.

As time goes on you will become aware of what life has to offer. By overcoming your reserve and helping someone in pain you may gain a wonderful friend. You may become friends through one small incident and then grow to really like each other. If you go through tough times with a friend, remembering the good times will help your friendship remain strong.

When we are disappointed, we may be quick to make assumptions. We assume the other person was being totally insensitive. Sometimes they don't seem to understand what's bothering us. Perhaps, though, they may be incapable of doing things differently. We increase the distance between ourselves and those around us because we mistakenly assume that everyone should see things as we do.

It's good to stop and look at what these judgments do to you. It's not a pretty sight! Have you stopped appreciating what you have and instead feel full of demands and complaints? Where did your gratitude go?

Okay! Time to straighten things out. Start realizing that every person has a different point of view, so use gentle words, and stop expecting everyone to agree with you instantly, all the time.

Each person has different preferences. Some people like to talk while others like to remain silent and listen. Some people want to go out and explore while others enjoy doing things at home. There are those who can't resist a book and will read a dictionary if that's the only volume available, while others who would rather construct something interesting.

The people you know may have different talents. You may keep your room spotless while someone else is always misplacing important papers. You may always remember what your teacher was wearing while your friend doesn't notice. Perhaps you can do an art project in half and hour while your friend can't draw at all. On the other hand, your friend might have no trouble putting thoughts down on paper while you spend hours on a one page essay.

People do things at a different pace. Some people speak and act quickly or spontaneously. Others need to plan in advance and a change in plans will upset them.

How do we respond to the imperfections of others? Do we have the urge to fix and change the people around us? Do we hope they will change by themselves? Is there a friend who always keeps you waiting or who cancels plans at the last minute? Do you tell yourself that this week she will be on time?

Have you ever given someone the benefit of the doubt? How does it feel? It may be a struggle at first. You may try to remain in control and to behave in a calm and proper manner, but it's hard not to let the annoyance show in your manner, and tone. It's difficult to remain gracious when you feel hurt. A voice inside may urge you to stick up for yourself. If you give others the benefit of the doubt you will feel relieved afterwards. You have accomplished something special. You can look back many years later and smile when you think about it. It's a lasting sweetness. It's a difficult endeavor that is worth the effort. One usually regrets an argument, but one never regrets a quarrel avoided. Arguments are usually worse than we expected them to be and result in a bitterness that lasts for a long time.

Forgive One Insult Every Day

Tante Raizy was relaxing on the terrace with her husband. Suddenly a downpour of water fell on them. It soaked her husband's head and shirt. Raizy got it on her sheitel. They yelled up to their upstairs neighbor, "What happened?"

The neighbor replied, "I didn't know you were sitting there," as she retreated through her door.

Later that day they faced the neighbor on the steps. They were hoping for an apology.

"You never sit in that corner. Why did you pick that corner just today?" the neighbor asked.

Tante Raizy didn't answer.

Later her husband asked, "Why did you keep quiet?"

"If I would scream and give her a piece of my mind, what would I have from it?"

Judaism encourages forgiving others unless there is a practical way that concrete damage can be restored or that lost money can be recovered. When we forgive others, God gives us a clean slate and forgives our sins. When we forgive others, and move forward, God helps us regain our loss.

Let go of resentment and move forward. Don't become paralyzed by anger. It will only intensify your loss. Don't get lost in self-pity; gather your resources and do all you can. Make the best of the situation.

✤ *Forgive and Let Go*

About ten years ago after a friendship ended in an ugly argument, I promised myself, "I'll never have another friend, because I never want to feel vulnerable to a painful loss again." After a week I cooled down and I was able to reach out again, but at first there was no one I wanted to see and nothing I wanted to do. Have you ever spent the day in a nothing cloud? You feel isolated in this fog and can't get through to yourself or to others. There are no openings, just bland whiteness. Your imagination, freedom of choice and ability to help yourself has closed down. You refuse to consider going forward because there is always a fear that you may have to say goodbye again. There is nothing to do, nothing you want, nothing you feel.

At that time, I found the following poem. It helped me forgive and let go.

Anyway

People are unreasonable, illogical and self-centered.
Love them anyway.

If you do good, people will accuse you of selfish ulterior motives.
Do good anyway.

If you are successful, you win false friends and true enemies.
Succeed anyway.

The good you do today will be forgotten tomorrow.
Do good anyway.

Honesty makes you vulnerable.
Be honest anyway.

What you spend years building may be destroyed overnight.
Build anyway.

People may attack you if you help them.
Help people anyway.

Give the world your best and you'll get kicked in the teeth.
Give the world your best
ANYWAY.

Together

Together. Sitting at the same table and in the same room. Sitting so close that when I look up I can look into your eyes. Yet are we sitting *together*?

Together. Standing and talking as the music plays. You compliment my dress and I compliment your jacket. We ask polite questions and pretend to hear the correct answers. However, are we standing *together*?

Together. Walking through the aisles of the grocery store. A little hand clutches mine. I worry if I'll be able to complete my shopping before the bus comes. You are telling me about red and yellow leaves that fall from the trees. Are we walking *together*?

The moments fly past. The opportunities to really connect surface and are lost again. Together means that two people communicate. When each one continues with daily life they have something to take along with them. That something may be remembered for only this week. That memory may also last a lifetime. Even an hour two people spend together can last a lifetime.

Every day has many hours and moments. Ask yourself tonight, "Which moments today did I spend *together* with another person?" Did I make a difference in someone's life today?

Together we can make many things better than they are now.

G.I.F.T.

Part 4

Triumph

What is an Accomplishment?

Something achieved
Something attained
Something that one worked hard for…

The real feeling of accomplishment
Comes only
When one
Has toiled
To conquer a seemingly unattainable goal.

Growing…
Maturing
Realizing the difference
Between fantasy and reality.

Acquiring persistence
The strength to cling
To your beliefs

Is there a connection?
You can only accomplish
After you've grown…
You grow
From your accomplishments.

Gitty Skolnick

Triumph

"First we have to believe, then we BELIEVE."
The Brisker Rav

Did you hear a gentle yet clear message today?

Is there a voice hidden within, urging you to do things in a better way?

There are goals that are just within our grasp if we reach for them on tiptoe. The prophets said about our time that there would be a hunger and a thirst, not for bread and water but to connect with the Almighty. In order for the yearning to be fulfilled it must be acknowledged. The silent spark must be attended to and supported by enthusiasm. Search each day to learn something meaningful. It doesn't have to be a lesson from a book. We learn lessons from the people we meet that are perhaps more vital and practical.

This is not the time to stop.

The stories in this book should encourage you to tell yourself that you can do it too.

You may not be able to see right at the moment how you can make a dream part of your reality. However, if you decide to open your eyes and to actively search, opportunities will definitely come your way. It's important to have goals prepared.

The Chofetz Chaim notes that the Torah stresses that we must walk in God's ways all the days. We must emulate Him by bestowing kindness and being compassionate. Every single day of our lives we must go out of our way to emulate God. Every single day of our lives we must go out of our way to do someone a favor (*Ahavas Chesed* Ch. 12 and *Love Your Neighbor*).

Doing someone a favor, gaining insight, becoming a better person makes one truly happy. This is not the time to stop. You can't afford the luxury of skepticism. Don't separate your ideals from your everyday life. When you believe you can triumph, you'll discover that all things are really possible.

- Don't get stuck in a setback, find new alternatives and move on.
- Do not settle for an ordinary existence. You can achieve something great.
- Remember to reach out to others.
- Do not take your cue from the crowd.
- Don't be discouraged by the obstacles in your way.

Unsung Heroes

Thankfulness can be compared to a magnet. Our appreciation attracts blessings from Hashem. When we acknowledge that our life is a gift we draw spiritual and material blessings from Hashem.

What is your image of triumph? Is it standing up to make a valedictory speech at graduation? Is it hitting a home run or winning a game of dodge ball? Perhaps you've watched others in their moments of triumph and wished that it could be you. We all can experience moments of triumph. However, triumph cannot be accessed instantly. The road to triumph is usually a long one and often there are obstacles in that path.

When we overcome challenges, big and small, the sense of victory and rejoicing are often unparalleled. Regardless of the outcome, learning to confront life's challenges is a vital aspect of becoming an adult and is essential for your future. Among other things, triumph culminates in thankfulness.

There are people I know with a variety of diseases and handicaps whom I consider "healthy." Their tone of voice makes it obvious that they are glad to meet you. They have decided to live each day vigorously. They have full-time jobs. They joyfully help others in their free moments. The lives of many people with handicaps are more "normal" than you would expect. They have triumphed over their limitations, and maintain a positive attitude.

What can I learn from these unsung heroes? I am convinced that the obstacles I face are easier than theirs. This means that I should surely stop griping and start smiling. I can find an extra ounce of strength when I'm fatigued and be patient when confronted by unreasonable people—it's really a matter of perspective. I can consider a host of possibilities if I minimize my limitations. My problems certainly are diminished when I consider the problems the unsung heroes overcome everyday.

All I have to do is recognize how fortunate I actually am. I tell myself if she can do_____ and _____ in spite of her disability, surely I can do something special too.

For Everything a Blessing

When I was an elementary school student in yeshiva — a Jewish Parochial school with both religious and secular studies — my classmates and I used to find amusing a sign that was posted just outside the bathroom. It was an ancient Jewish blessing, commonly referred to as the Asher Yatzar benediction, that was supposed to be recited after one relieved oneself. For grade school children, there could be nothing more strange or ridiculous than to link the act of defecation with holy words that mentioned God's name.

It took me several decades to realize the wisdom that lay behind this blessing that was composed by Abayei, a fourth century Babylonian rabbi.

Abayei's blessing is contained in the Talmud, an encyclopedic work of Jewish law and lore. On page 120 (Berachos 60b) of the ancient text it is written: Abayei said, when one comes out of a bathroom he should say: "Blessed is He who has formed man in wisdom and created in him many orifices and cavities. It is obvious and known before Your throne of glory that if one of them were to be ruptured or one of them blocked, it would be impossible for a man to survive and stand before You. Blessed are You that heals all flesh and does wonders."

It is one thing, however, to post these signs and it is quite another to realistically expect teenagers to have the maturity to realize the wisdom of the need for reciting a 1,500-year-old-blessing related to bodily functions.

It was not until my second year of medical school that I first began to understand the appropriateness of this short prayer. I began to no longer take for granted the normalcy of my trips to the bathroom. Instead I began to realize how many things had to operate just right for these minor interruptions of my daily routine to run smoothly.

I thought of Abayei and his blessing. I recalled my days at yeshiva and remembered how silly that sign outside the bathroom had seemed. But after seeing patients whose lives revolved around their dialysis machines and others with catheters I realized how wise the rabbi had been.

I began to recite Abayei's blessing. At first I had to go back to my siddur, the Jewish prayer book, to get the text right. With repetition—and there are many opportunities for a human to get to know this blessing well—I could recite it fluently and with sincerity and understanding.

Over the years, reciting the Asher Yatzar has become for me an opportunity to offer thanks, not just for my excretory organs, but for my overall good health. The text, after all, refers to catastrophic consequences of the rupture or obstruction of any bodily structure. Could Abayei have foreseen that blockage of the coronary artery would lead to the commonest cause of death in industrialized countries some 16 centuries later?

I have often wondered if other people also yearn for some way to express gratitude for their good health. Physicians especially who are exposed daily to the ravages that illness can wreak, must sometimes feel the need to express thanks for being well.

There was one unforgettable patient whose story reinforced the truth and beauty of the Asher Yatzar for me forever. Josh was a 20-year-old student who sustained an unstable fracture of his third and fourth cervical vertebrae in a motor vehicle crash. He nearly died from his injury and required breathing support. He was initially totally quadriplegic but for weak flexion of his right biceps.

A long and difficult period of stabilization and rehabilitation followed. There were promising signs of recovery over the first few months that came suddenly and unexpectedly: movement of a finger here, flexion of a toe there, return of sensation here. With incredible courage, hard work and an excellent physical therapist, Josh improved day by day. In time, and after what seemed like a miracle, he was able to walk slowly with a leg brace and a cane.

But Josh continued to require intermittent catheterization. I knew only too well the problem and perils this young man would face for the rest of his life. The urologists were very pessimistic *about his chances for not requiring catheterization. They had not seen this occur after a spinal cord injury of this severity.*

Then the impossible happened. I was there the day Josh no longer required a urinary catheter. I thought of Abayei's Asher Yatzar prayer. Pointing out that I could not imagine a more meaningful scenario for its recitation, I suggested to Josh, who was also a yeshiva graduate, that he say the prayer. He agreed. As he recited the ancient brachah, tears welled in my eyes. Josh is my son.

By Keneth M. Prager M.D.
New York, NY

Reprinted from the Journal of the American Medical Association, May 28, 1987

Thinking of Others

Obstacles are difficult, but they don't have to hold us back if we believe in ourselves. It's tempting to just sit on the side and watch others toil and accomplish, yet if we get up and act we often surprise ourselves. If we have confidence and think that we can reach a particular goal—we can.

This is a story of an unsung hero who has suffered a setback and yet emerged as a successful adult. There are examples in your own community. If you ask these unsung heroes how they succeeded you will hear stories of struggle and persistence.

Isn't someone with a handicap entitled to focus only on him or herself? All their emotional and physical stamina are needed just to face things that most of us so easily take for granted—like dressing, eating and standing. Each of these activities is an insurmountable mountain to be climbed and coped with if you are handicapped. This is the life and story of Brocha Tzemel, a wonderful woman faced with the devastating disease of multiple sclerosis. multiple sclerosis is a progressive degenerative disease that affects the nerves and muscles. Often multiple sclerosis can cause vision problems, poor motor control and trouble in speaking.

Brocha first began losing strength in her feet. Consequently, she concentrated on her hands and became a talented seamstress. She even gave sewing classes. Then Brocha saw that even her hands were getting weaker. Instead of becoming bitter and helpless she looked to see what she could still do.

Brocha realized that she still had the gift of speech. Brocha decided to use this gift for making shidduchim, especially for people who are disabled.

One day Brocha was rushed to the hospital. She had lost her power of speech. The doctors said that nothing would bring it back. Nevertheless, Brocha had hope. She trusted that Hashem would help her because she fervently believed that she had to continue with her shidduchim.

The doctors didn't want Brocha to leave the hospital. They thought she was close to the end. Brocha insisted that she return to her own house and her husband managed to convince the doctors. That night as Brocha lay awake she promised Hashem that she would do everything she could to help other people, especially those who were truly desperate. Brocha then rolled her chair over to the mirror and started to talk.

Brocha continued her matchmaking, taking on the most difficult cases. She would remind her clients that she was not a magician, just God's messenger trying to help them.

Brocha never gave up. When she couldn't do things with her hands she found another way to be helpful and productive. She is a wonderful example for all of us. We must develop our attributes to their full potential and be thankful for all we have.

Sora Hindy S.

Every time someone depicts how they succeeded you will also find a setback in their account. There is no such thing as a person who has **never** failed at anything. We usually focus on our exciting accomplishments and overlook the struggles, but the struggles are there. No human being is always a champion; each of us has to overcome adversity. We admire these people specifically because they triumphed over their difficulties.

They did not give up until a solution was found for their specific problem. Those victories were not achieved overnight, but rather it took years of attempts and failures and trying again until they succeeded. We feel hopeful and inspired when we realize how hard even ordinary tasks were for some people, yet they would not give up.

Help and Support Someone

Sometimes a friend needs your support, advice and comfort. Look within and you will find the way to reveal the strength of your friendship.

A friendship that lasts is built on caring. Close your eyes and recall an experience in which you felt secure and cherished. Feel all the sensations of that memory. You want to give that warmth to your friend.

Even when your friend's situation changes you are there to help. True friendship means being there to provide encouragement.

Rejoice in the miracle of your mutual understanding.

> *I recently received a degree for being an expert encourager. A close friend of mines had Epstein-Barre, throughout the entire tenth grade. It was my job to constantly try to cheer her up. After a hard day at school I'd call or stop by her house to lift her spirits. It's not easy to miss an entire year of school. I'd walk in to her house and she'd be sitting on the couch. She'd greet me with the brightest smile and the loudest hello. At those times, I'd forget who was supposed to be encouraging who.*
>
> *Encouraging my friend was a boost for me. I felt a burst of gratitude and thankfulness to Hashem for my boring, normal life. My friend pulled through her illness and now she's back in school. I'm sure the fact that she didn't see her illness as a dark tunnel but as a challenge helped a lot.*
>
> *Malky G.*

- Encourage and support your friends and family in good times and bad.
- Talk to close friends about things that matter.
- Learn from a Torah book with a friend on a regular basis.
- Tell each of your friends three sincere compliments this week.

Difficult Decisions

•❖ *Stage Fright*

I was asked to sing a solo at my eighth grade graduation. Although everyone kept encouraging me and telling me that I would do a good job, I was really scared. Once when I sang in the past I had a terrible case of stage fright. Since then I get nervous every time I stand before an audience.

I was scared that I would not be able to sing at the graduation. I wanted to ask my teacher to give the solo to someone else, but I was embarrassed.

I thought about how nervous I'd feel throughout the graduation ceremony. My heart would be beating wildly, my hands sweating, my blood pressure rising and my voice shaking.

On graduation day I finally made my decision. I asked my teacher if I could share my solo with another girl. We would be a duet. My teacher agreed.

I felt relaxed throughout the graduation. I knew I would not sing alone and I was no longer nervous. I enjoyed everything about the graduation.

This challenge taught me that I can figure out a solution to a problem. Once I had mustered the courage I was able to proceed. I was smiling so hard on the way home that I thought my cheeks would stretch. I feel that since I was able to do this duet, I can do anything.

Malkie S.

•❖ *Blizzard*

Do you remember the famous blizzard of '96? Four feet of snow fell in our neighborhood; in some places even more. We were homebound from Sunday to Wednesday.

A neighbor came around the corner to my door. "Can you come with me to the nursing home? My mother was there yesterday and she saw that there were no volunteers to help the nurses feed the patients because of the bad weather," she said.

We went and found that there were many residents with no one helping them.

I'm proud of my friend. She looked at a challenge and did it. Together, we turned the situation into something good.

Miriam G.

❧ Stop and Think

"Come on, let's ditch class."
"Yeah, I hate math class!"
"Come on, Anikke, let's go!"

Wait! Do I want to do this? Is this good for me? No! I don't want to ditch class.

Sometimes you get in a situation when everyone is doing something but you have to stop and think—Do I want to do this?

You have to think for yourself. If you don't think about what you really want, you aren't going to be happy.

Annike S. Fox

❧ Moving to a New Place

After my Bas Mitzvah my parents told me the news: We were going to move from our lovely house in Oregon, to Seattle, Washington.

I took the news of moving to Washington extremely hard. I ran upstairs, crying all the way. I didn't want to leave all my friends and family. I would be going to a place where I knew no one. I called all my friends one by one to tell them the news. I spoke lightly and said that I would be okay, until it came to the last phone call.

I was calling someone who I did not know very well. I broke into tears again. My friend told me that she would miss me, but that Washington was only a state over and a phone call away. She told me that I was lucky to move because I would make more friends.

Now after living here for a year, I see how she was right. I came here with the intention of making friends and so I did. I have found life to be pleasant and back to normal again. Every so often I go back and visit, and I still miss the life I once had in Oregon. Those memories will always be with me, but I learned that you must always be willing to move on and try hard to do what is right.

Jennifer Miller

Thoughtfulness

There is a rule in our school that you can't have an open drink in the hallways. I didn't think that this applied to walking from lunch to class. In the class that I was heading to, the teacher threw away my pop, yet let another girl keep hers. Why? I was so upset, so I went and told the principal how I felt.

The next day, I had another open pop after lunch. (The principal hadn't got back to me yet to tell me what I should do.) This time a different teacher yelled at me and threw away my pop. Now I was even more upset, so again I went and told the principal. He understood my problem and found a solution.

I went to see him right after tefillah. He had gotten me an open/close water bottle. I greatly appreciated his thoughtfulness. This situation taught me an important trait — thoughtfulness. It's

Triumph ☐ 181

easy to tell people what they should do. Doing something about the situation is totally different and certainly more helpful. When people just talk you feel it's your problem alone and not theirs. Instead my principal helped me with my problem. Giving me the water bottle showed that he understands and cares about us.

Miri Azose

•❖ *A Personal Prayer to God, Master of the Universe*

You have always been there for me when I needed You. Always watching, always caring, always listening. I really appreciate everything that You have done for me. For example, You provided me with wonderful parents and a nice brother. When my family needed money, You made sure that we had food, clothing, housing and a Jewish education. Now I ask You one more favor. My great-grandmother is getting older. She has always been around when I needed someone to talk to. At this point I need her more than anything. I am about to enter high school and I don't have a lot of friends. Together we chat on the phone, and she helps me see things on a higher level or from a different side. Please let her stay. Keep her healthy and full of fun. We often go out to dinner. We talk about life, school and other topics. She always manages to find something funny in something serious. She makes me laugh and smile with her. Let her be here for me. I love her. Thank You.

Jennifer M.

Sarah's Story

This is the story of a midget named Sarah. You are right, she does look different, but to me she looks just like any other person. That's because when I look at her, I see what's **inside** and in my opinion that's what counts most.

QUESTION: *Did people ever stare or make fun of you?*

SARAH: Throughout my life, especially in the younger grades, it was hard to make friends. When children see someone different they don't know how to react so they just laugh or stare.

QUESTION: *How did you deal with this?*

SARAH: When I was little, I used to feel sorry for myself and cry. As I got older I realized if they make fun of me, it's their stigma, not mine.

QUESTION: *Are there any special privileges you feel you get because you are short?*

SARAH: Oh, definitely. First, because I'm considered handicapped, my husband's allowed to park just about anywhere. Second, because they don't have mature clothing in my size I have to get custom-made clothing. My neighbor is a seamstress. She makes me everything. All we have to do is give her material. Since it's so convenient and relatively inexpensive I'm constantly getting new clothing. Doesn't that sound great?

QUESTION: *How did you cope when you were a suitable age for marriage and your friends were getting married one by one?*

SARAH: I think my parents were nervous and worried, but they were careful to cover it up. I started getting worried when I realized most of my friends were married with kids. Then one night we got a phone call from my brother-in-law in New York. He heard of a boy who came from a great family who also happened to be "short." Soon after we met and got married. This April will be our sixth anniversary.

QUESTION: *What message would you like to share with the reader?*

SARAH: Just appreciate what you have. It's terrible that people only seem to appreciate what they have when it's almost taken away.

Feige's Story

QUESTION: *How do you communicate with hearing people?*

FEIGE: In school I was taught how to lip-read and sign. Some people find it harder to understand me than others. But after 8 years with a speech therapist, my speech is passable. Most people can understand me if they try.

QUESTION: *How would you describe your early life?*

FEIGE: Well, I am very thankful to my parents and wonderful siblings. They are all loving and patient people. But life was still very hard for me. I always felt like an outcast to my neighbors and cousins. I hated it when people would stare at me because my speech sounded different. It was also very frustrating not to be understood by my own parents or siblings. At the Shabbos table when someone would tell a joke and my whole family would be laughing, I had to wait for someone to explain it to me. By the time I'd get the joke it wasn't funny anymore. This is just an example of the things that hearing people take for granted that is torture for a deaf person.

QUESTION: *Tell us about how you cope with your children.*

FEIGE: I've got to give a big thank you to technology. For example, how do I hear my child cry? There is a microphone by the childrens' beds; every loud sound the child makes causes a light to flash or my bed to vibrate. The phone is one long flash and the doorbell is three quick flashes. My oldest child is four years old and he communicates with me by using sign language and reading lips. It was hard for me to read his tiny lips at first so I taught him sign language. In school he is like every other child. My daughter was having some trouble speaking . We have arranged for a speech therapist and hope her language skills will improve. As for sign language, she knows a lot more sign language than actual speech.

QUESTION: *Do you have a job now? What do you do?*

FEIGE: My husband is the president of a company called Hear More. It is a company that manufactures things to help the deaf and hearing impaired. For example, he manufactures the special devices that detect sound and cause flashing lights. They also manufacture hearing aids and TTY. I am a manager of this company. I communicate with the deaf people who come in to purchase these devices to help them in everyday life. I am happy to be helping people get these things that I never had as a kid. I had to rely on my parents and siblings to tell me everything. Right now I feel very independent and it's important that every deaf person should feel that way too.

There are no words to describe how much I look up to my sister. She has taught me so much and I am inspired by the way she never gives up. The distress of not being understood and the feeling that others were ridiculing her never caused her to give up. Often my mother said, "Feige, don't try so hard." However, my sister never did anything without giving it her best.

Shoes

Spina bifida is a congenital spinal defect. Most patients will have some degree of weakness in the legs. Many children who are able to learn to walk will require braces. Hydrocephalus frequently accompanies spina bifida. It is a condition in which too much cerebrospinal fluid is produced. To prevent continuing fluid buildup and pressure on the brain, children with spina bifida must have a shunt inserted. It is surgically inserted to drain fluid from the head to the abdomen.

Dina T. was born with spina bifida. She is able to walk with only a slight limp. It's difficult for her to go up stairs and carry heavy objects. Her story of triumph is inspiring. She is married, runs a home and has a healthy child.

QUESTION: *What are some challenges that you remember facing as a young child?*

DINA: I walked with a limp. Children would see me and innocently ask, "Why do you walk like that?" Kids are curious and it's normal for them to ask questions. However, it took time for me to take the questions in stride.

QUESTION: *Did your family treat you differently from your other siblings?*

DINA: My wonderful parents and family treated me like a regular child. That was the best thing ever. I was always like anyone else. I was accepted. Everyone did a Shabbos job. Maybe I cut paper towels instead of vacuuming (because that was too difficult for me physically), but that didn't matter. I didn't feel different.

QUESTION: *What can you tell us about your shunt?*

DINA: I had my first shunt inserted when I was three months old. It was adjusted when I was three years old and again when I was 14. I was growing, but the shunt doesn't grow, so it had to be replaced. It's good that I'm short because otherwise I would have had to have my shunt replaced more frequently.

QUESTION: *Do you remember any uplifting incidents?*

DINA: When I was a child, I had to wear orthopedic shoes because they gave my feet much more support. Every year I went to Reb Moshe Feinstein for a *berachah*. On my visit when I was ten years old, Reb Moshe asked me, "What do you want?" I told him that I wanted to get rid of my ugly shoes. Reb Moshe gave me a *berachah* and I left.

During that spring, my friends in school played jump rope. I would sit on the side and watch. One day, one of my friends come over and asked me why I wasn't playing. I told her that I didn't know how to jump, and besides it would be too hard for me. "How do you know?" my friend asked. "You haven't tried. If you try to jump, I'll give you a dollar." I hesitated. Then she took out another dollar and said, "If you jump I'll give you two dollars." That did it! I tried and I jumped!

The whole school celebrated. The principal called my mother and grandfather to tell them the good news. It was a like a *Yom Tov* for my family. We had doughnuts for dessert that night.

A few days later, it was then two weeks after I had visited Reb Moshe, I went to the doctor for a check-up. In the doctor's office, I saw a kid who had feet that were totally slanted in, yet he was wearing velcro sneakers. (Velcro sneakers were very cool in those days.)

When I went in to see the doctor, I asked why I could not wear sneakers. He asked, "What exercise have you been doing recently?"

"I have learned how to jump rope," I replied. The doctor looked at me like I was crazy. He took a rope out of his drawer to test me, to see if it was true. My father held one end and he held the other, and I jumped! That very day, I went to buy my first pair of normal sneakers! I wanted to call Reb Moshe at that moment to tell him, "Hashem answered your blessing!"

QUESTION: *What are some tips you can give others who are challenged with a difficulty or handicap?*

DINA: A person must realize that every individual was created with different strengths and weaknesses. One person can't draw and another can't do something else. No one is perfect. It's just that some flaws are more noticeable that others. Disabled means not able and everyone is not able to do something. You just have to be your best at what you can do. Once I knew that I was much better off.

After interviewing Dina I learned that in every difficult situation, there's always good. We have to open our eyes to see the good. Because Dina is short, kids made fun of her. After interviewing Dina I learned a better way to understand the term "disabled." Accepting the fact that no one is able to do <u>everything</u> helps one view her shortcomings in a different way. She taught me to do your best and look for the good in everything.

Leah Malka B.

Overcoming Disappointment

Sometimes in our lives we face a disappointment. The sooner we say goodbye to our unrealized expectations, the easier it will be to find new alternatives and move on.

If you wanted to go on a trip but your friend cancels, you've got to say goodbye to those plans. If a job interview fails, you've got to say goodbye to that job. If your best friend finds someone else and ignores you, you've got to say goodbye to that friend. If you want to walk home from school with someone new but she says no, you've got to say goodbye for now. If your best friend moves to Israel, you've got to say goodbye. If you lose money, you've got to say goodbye to the money. When you graduate elementary school, you've got to say goodbye to your old school.

Long goodbyes aren't helpful. If you can say goodbye to whatever is not working for you, you will then be free to discover a better alternative. Usually, you will see new possibilities right away.

> *On a Sunday morning about five years ago I joined my father for his morning walk to pick up the Sunday Times. We were in a little town in the Catskill Mountains and the scenery was relaxing and awe inspiring. Suddenly our pleasant interlude was interrupted. My father tripped at an uneven place in the road. I felt like I had stopped breathing. There my father lay, sprawled on the road. I helped him up and noticed that his knee was bruised. "Should I call Mommy to come get us with the car?" I asked.*
>
> *"What in the world would we need the car for?" my father responded impatiently. "I'm fine. We are just going to keep on going and get the paper as we planned."*
>
> *We walked some more. My father limped near me, smiling and chatting as if nothing had happened. "I want you to know something, Roiza, God helps one who has fallen. I've seen it happen again and again in my life. As long as you don't give up, you can triumph over many setbacks. I'll tell you a parable about it.*

"A gang of thieves is planning a robbery. One of the group enters the store, takes some merchandise and flees. He is hoping that the merchant will chase him and abandon the store, leaving it unguarded so that the rest of his friends can plunder it completely. The smart merchant understands this ploy. He says to himself: 'Let the thief keep what he grabbed.' He refuses to abandon his post and continues to do business, keeping a careful lookout. He knows that the loss will eventually be recovered, and that he will still earn a profit."

The merchant in this story kept a clear head and a hopeful outlook. He knew that even though he had lost something, the misfortune was now in the past. He would not be foolish enough to "jump in" after the loss and thereby cause himself more worry and depression. He allowed bygones to be bygones, secure in the knowledge that he could recoup his deficit and continue his endeavors with strength.

This is not just a parable. It is something you can do, too.
Did it ever happen to you?

A Quiet Breakthrough

I've traveled by plane many times but I've never been a first class passenger. I've heard that first class passengers enjoy certain privileges. They don't have to wait on line, a chauffeur picks them up in a limousine from their home, and their seats are larger. It's the airlines' way of generating new business. Airlines also extend the royal treatment by giving each first class passenger a small tote bag that is decorated with the airline's logo and filled with treats. This bag may include a plastic pocket comb and brush, a bag of smoked almonds, a tiny package of Wet Ones and a sewing kit. I know because my uncle gave one of these bags to my children when they visited him.

In our family, a plane trip is a special occasion. Family members include money with their wishes for a safe flight. It isn't for the traveler to keep; but to be given to charity upon arrival at the destination. This way the traveler is a *Shaliach Mitzvah,* an emissary for a good deed. The Talmud says that such an emissary has Divine protection.

During the blizzard of 1993 I felt more nervous than usual about boarding a plane to visit my parents. I watched the mountains of snow forming on Sunday and wondered if I would go on this trip at all. The radio said that it was the worst weather in a decade. On Monday, all offices in Manhattan were closed. Would the airport be open at all on Wednesday? I called the airline several times on Tuesday and was assured that all planes were expected to take off according to schedule. However, when I woke up on Wednesday and stared out at the huge snowdrifts everywhere, I felt quite apprehensive.

What if the plane is delayed? What if it can't take off because of gusting winds? The worries and uncertainties kept creeping back and pulling me down. I hadn't slept well and I felt the fatigue. I figured my entire day would be difficult since I was feeling so tired. I didn't feel exactly hopeful. Actually, I fantasized that I would cancel the trip and go back to sleep but I had a non-refundable ticket.

The phone rang just as I was finishing my bowl of cereal. It was my niece. "Can I come over now? Matis made cards and pictures for Zeidy and Bubby that I want to send along with you."

"Sure," I replied, "I've been up since 6 A.M. I can't wait to give the pictures to them."

Five minutes later the door bell rang. My niece had her hands full. One hand held the big manila envelope with her son's artwork. The other hand held a large yellow gift bag that was covered with cheerful balloons.

We sat down together at the kitchen table. "The gift bag is for you. I hope you enjoy your flight," my niece explained. I opened the bag and peeked inside.

I noticed three newspapers first. "I really had Zeidy in mind when I bought those." My niece confessed. "I know he always wants the most recent Jewish newspapers and you can't get those in Florida. But you can read them on the plane ride."

I pushed the newspapers aside and found other treats. There were two danishes, two black and white cookies and several chocolate bars. Under that layer there was a small Tupperware container of fresh fruit salad. I saw chunks of cantaloupe and strawberries and smiled. There was so much love in this bag! In the corner my niece still found room for two packets of hot cocoa mix and one small envelope. The envelope had the words "for charity" on the outside, and a five-dollar bill inside. Now I was a *Shaliach Mitzvah*.

My niece's early morning pre-flight visit helped me focus on hopeful feelings and relax. She helped me regain my usual optimism. It would all be fine and I'd have a chance to visit my parents and give them pleasure. My niece reminded me there was a better way. Her thoughtful nurturing was the impetus I needed. I couldn't make the snow go away, but I could control my thinking. I could feel hopeful by seeing past the apparent problem to the good in the situation. I could locate and listen to the hopeful voice within. I realized the value of a good attitude.

That morning was a quiet breakthrough for me. I had always heard that it was important to have a good attitude. Now I saw that it could be done.

Thanks, Chaya Sara, you made me feel even better than if I were traveling first class.

I'm Starving

Haven't we all tried to watch what we eat, keep track of our portion size, write down our food intake or, in one word, diet? If you must fit into to a particular dress for a special occasion, you might feel under pressure to be more scrupulous about your food intake. What if you cheat on your diet? You might feel foolish but you'll probably take it in stride, shrug your shoulders and start all over again.

Dieting is a trend that is usually harmless. Sometimes, however, one gets too absorbed in wanting to be perfect. Whether it's in the quest for the perfect figure, the perfect grade or the perfect face—obsession can cause one to become her own enemy. We cannot allow our self-image to depend on a dress size or number. An individual might cut herself off from someone or something. They might cut themselves off from their own life force—from the source of wisdom and power within.

It took a lot of courage for Shira* to share this story with others. She challenges us with several difficult questions. Does our society put too much emphasis on weight and appearance? Where does this obsession lead? The potential for serious misunderstanding is astonishing. Shira shares her story in the hope that she can help others avoid the terrible pain she experienced.

I lived through torture—terrible, horrible torture. The cruel twist to my suffering was that it was self-inflicted. I did it to myself, but it was your fault. It was your fault and the fault of every person in this world who is obsessed with thinness. You caused me to reach the end of the cliff. It's fortunate that I didn't jump. I was on the brink of becoming anorexic and it was a daily struggle to make sure I didn't slip, lose my balance and fall off the edge.

---

* Name has been changed.

I was away working as an Arts and Crafts counselor when it began. It started out as a normal diet. After four weeks I had lost fifteen pounds. My skirts got looser and I was extremely happy. However, each day I started eating less and less until I was barely eating at all. I was hungry when I woke up, hungry when I went to sleep and hungry all the time in between. Without being aware of it I was developing a psychological aversion to food. I would sit on the grass in the sunshine and dream about eating a soft chocolate danish. I was always thinking about food. It followed me wherever I went.

What was a typical day in my life like? I woke up in the morning and there was a dull ache in my stomach—a cry from my body, a plea for food, for some sustenance. I would quietly sneak into the infirmary to weigh myself. If I had lost a pound or two from the day before I was delirious with happiness. If I didn't lose or if I had gained a pound my heart broke. Slowly I would trudge down the hill to the casino, where everyone met for Shacharis. I didn't have the strength to run—I walked in a slow shuffle. It was a test of pure determination to keep on walking on the path until I reached the casino. I entered the casino breathing hard—trying to regain my strength. Had anyone noticed?

The day dragged on. I bought a diet soda for lunch. Overcome by hunger pangs, I could not resist the temptation to eat an apple that was served as an afternoon snack. After I ate it, I felt pangs of guilt assaulting me. I shouted at myself, "Why did you just eat that?" The same thing happened every time I let a morsel of food pass through my lips.

The campers were always complaining it was hot, yet I'd sit in my seat shivering. I was always cold. I helped the girls with their arts and crafts project. I really enjoyed showing the girls how to sand the wood, stain and laquer it and then attach the beautiful Aishes Chayil poem. However, when someone walked past with a chocolate bar or a bag of potato chips, it was hard to watch her eat it.

I walked out of the bunkhouse chattering and laughing with my friends. Sometimes I felt dizzy and then a dark blackness crept up on me. The darkness started at the edge of my irises and slowly spread over the rest of my eyes. I quickly ran and sat down under the nearest tree and took deep breaths. Slowly the heavy veil of darkness dissipated. I was careful to glue a grin to my face as I sat breathing deeply. Would anyone guess how I really felt behind that carefree smile?

I ate two rice cakes as I rested before supper. At supper it was easy to surreptitiously throw most of the contents of my plate into the garbage. I resolutely ignored my stomach's angry rumbling.

I lay alone on my bed and cried. I cried for myself—for my suffering and my obstinacy. Why couldn't I just let myself eat like a normal person? I begged Hashem, "Please help me through this!" I fell asleep, the tears drying on my cheeks.

Boruch Hashem I was able to overcome this affliction and suffer no lasting effects.

The other day I noticed a girl who seems to be going through the same torture I went through. I know the helplessness and despair she is experiencing. I wish I could help her. What can I do to help? I wish I knew.

Every one of us can help by deciding not to place such a disproportionate emphasis on physical appearance. The inside of a person is infinitely more valuable.

I am so grateful that I didn't take the plunge off the cliff but what can guarantee that others won't?

Isn't it incredible? She stood at the edge of the cliff, yet she stepped back in time. Everyone can identify with Shira's need to fit in. We all strive for perfection to some degree. However, in her desperate need to be perfect, Shira brought agony upon herself and risked her health. Now her heart beats calmly again. Her life is orderly and predictable.

Shira is a happy teenager. She hardly ever walks alone. Her friends and family think she's wonderful. Did they realize that she was going through a hard and scary interval?

Dieting became problematic because it was done to the extreme and led to self-inflicted pain. Shira has one motivation in sharing her story. She has a deep, delicate concern that this suffering should not occur to others. Our actions do make a difference.

Do we use our appearance to measure our self-worth? Is our identity linked to the way we look? Does success depend on how beautiful we are on the outside? King Solomon wisely declared thousands of years ago that the beauty that lies inside our heart, mind and soul is our real success.

We can use our closeness to Hashem and our acts of kindness to express who we are. Let's give each other strength and courage instead of comparing, competing and judging. Instead of trying to feel superior by looking better than our peers, let's become better people by being loyal friends.

The Specialness of "Ordinary" Days

Plain, ordinary days are a gift. When you choose to view every day as a gift you open yourself fully to each moment and each situation. You give everything and hold nothing back.

You can decide to make your life deeply fulfilling. You have the power to find your purpose today. That power lies in realizing that each ordinary day is really great.

- Find the courage to bring your idealism with you wherever you go.
- Find the courage to radiate cheerful encouragement to whomever you meet.
- Say Shehecheyanu—not only a few times a year, but on ordinary days as well.

❧ *Anxiously Waiting*

Last year my aunt came to America to have a tumor removed from her brain. She was not sure if it was cancerous or not. The surgery was in Pittsburgh. She went with her husband and son.

It was difficult to be far away. I wanted to be nearby and know what was going on immediately. I didn't want to be sitting near the phone waiting for it to ring. I will never forget the phone call.

My sister picked up the phone. I saw her start to cry. I was sure that something was wrong. I began screaming, "What happened? What happened?"

She said, "Everything is O.K. These are tears of joy, not sorrow."

The tension we felt until we knew the outcome made me realize how great it is to have plain, ordinary days. You just want to say Shehecheyanu and thank Hashem that everyone is fine.

Sara R.

∾ My Father in Heaven

When I cry, He comforts. When I laugh, He delights in my happiness. When I sigh, He understands my disappointment. My Father helps me through the trials and tribulations of this challenging journey called life.

When I was young, it was to Him that I confided my fears of new places, things and ideas. When I grew older, it was to Him that I begged for health and happiness. It was with Him that I shared my yearning for security and comfort.

Many times a day, I cry out to Him and He is all encompassing. My Father enables me to live a meaningful life. His love for me is boundless. I try my hardest to reciprocate the kindness He showers upon me. Through my whole life He is there for me. Thank you, my dear Father — Father in Heaven.

Chaya L.

On Overcoming Fear

"One does not discover new lands without consenting to lose sight of the shore for a very long time."
Andre Gide

Our confidence grows as we practice and prepare, yet we are never completely ready to dive into a new experience.

The first attempt calls for all our courage. Despite a palpitating heart and a shaky stomach, we push ourselves and face our fears.

Afterwards we may say, "I've never felt like such a winner!" A triumphant joy envelops us that feels too wonderful for words.

Despite my fear of the pool, my mother decided to give me swimming lessons. "When I was in first grade I started taking swimming lessons and I eventually became experienced at doing the basic swimming strokes.

There I was, a terrified third grader, standing in front of the crystal blue pool. I was taking the very frightening deep water test. My mother and a lifeguard were present. It was toward the end of the summer and I wanted to go home from the country feeling relieved and accomplished. I wanted to know that I had passed the test. There was one slight problem—I was scared to jump in the water and it was a requirement to pass the test.

"Come on, you can do it !" my mother said encouragingly.

"No, I can't!" I whined. "I'll go down when I jump and I'll never come back up!"

"Nonsense," exclaimed my mother. "The lifeguard is standing right here with her pole. She's ready to save you if you need it."

"I don't care," I replied, trembling. "I'll pass the test next year."

"Come on, don't disappoint us," my mother pleaded. "You will be the only one your age who didn't pass the test."

I returned my gaze to the water. I couldn't see the floor of the pool, because the water was so deep. I could feel the tension in me. My heartbeat sounded like galloping horses. The chlorine smell penetrated my insides. I gave one more look at the pool. "I'll do it," I said in a determined voice. I didn't want to be called the "neb" because I didn't pass the deep water test. I inched slowly to the edge of the pool. I shut my eyes as tight as a vacuum pack. I counted until three in my head and then stopped again. "Come on, you can do it!" encouraged the life guard. One two three jump! I did it! From under the water I could hear my mother clapping. I passed the rest of my test easily.

Whoever said beginnings are easy? Now I love swimming and jumping in is as easy as pie. The beginning was hard but the outcome was well worth it. Next time you are faced with a hard situation, grin and bear it—it will turn out well.

G.H.

Going Forward

Children have a great degree of innocent confidence. They are truly certain that their prayers are heard and reach the heavens. They constantly strive to experiment, learn and achieve their goals. They plunge ahead and are confident that they will make an impact.

When we get older we may spend an inordinate amount of time thinking before we act. At times this may produce effective results, but other times this keeps us from simply taking action. We may not understand why everyone else doesn't appreciate our perfectionism.

Sometimes it's good to remember what it was like to simply carry out a plan on the spur of the moment. It's good to become successfully involved with the hands-on aspect of helping others. If it feels right, get up and go.

~~~

One of my first memories is of a rainy day, when I was three years old. We lived in an apartment building with four other Jewish families. On this particular dreary day my little playmates and I were sitting on the steps in our building, bored stiff. The huge yard outside was beckoning us to come play, it was so lonely. But our mothers had told us that we must not go out in the rain. So there we were, brainstorming and trying to come up with something that appealed to our young minds.

I came up with a brilliant suggestion. "I have the best idea," I informed my friend, "why don't we daven for all the sick people?"

My friends agreed that this was the best idea yet. "But we don't know how to," one of my friends, Rochel Leah, pointed out practically.

"We sure do," I retorted in my best teacher voice. "We can say "Ani Maamin Berefuah Shleima!" We positioned ourselves more comfortably on the stairs and began to sing. Pretty soon the entire building resounded in song and prayer.

Miri G.

Simple Things
I Can Appreciate

1. Spending time with friends
2. Hearing the recess bell
3. Seeing the sunset
4. Listening to music
5. Talking on the telephone
6. Smelling Challah baking in the oven
7. Looking at photographs
8. Seeing the shimmering clear water of the seashore
9. Seeing color
10. Getting from one place to another easily
11. Seeing the breathtaking view from a mountaintop
12. Waking up to the sound of birds chirping in the morning
13. Seeing a blanket of white, newly fallen snow covering everything on a winter morning
14. Hearing an inspiring tefillah on a holiday
15. Watching and hearing young children playing
16. Seeing a flock of birds flying south in a V-formation
17. Listening to young children reciting Aleph Beis
18. Watching the waves of the ocean crash against the rocks
19. Seeing the faces of the people in my family
20. Seeing my sisters race to the swings in the park and hearing their laughter
21. Seeing the deep blue sky dotted with seven small clouds above me
22. Seeing buds blossoming on all the trees once again, after a cold winter

A Note to the Reader

The main reason I have this page in here is so readers everywhere can share their thoughts, questions, ideas and stories. My teen readers have been the most enthusiastic writers. I will try my very best to respond.

Roiza Weinreich
625 Avenue L
Brooklyn, N.Y. 11230

About the Author

Roiza Devorah Weinreich is the bestselling author of *There Will Never Be Another You, In Joy, A Happier You* and *W.H.A.T. Can Relieve Stress*. Each book gives you the feeling that you are visiting with the author. There are questions, interviews, stories and exercise pages to help you feel that you are a participant in a workshop as you read the book. Roiza has designed and presented practical workshops based on Torah principles and true success stories for 15 years. She is a teacher at Bais Yaakov High School. She also speaks at school and tzedakah gatherings.

YA Fic WE
A Gift for Teens
Ideas and stories to keep you going
Weinreich Roiza

Mesor... ...ications, ltd
440. Second Avenue